Made in the USA
Monee, IL
12 November 2026

b523ead4-a1dc-42e1-88b8-045ffe74d7ddR01

Digital Marketing
for Mental Health

Adrienne Wilkerson

Co-Founder + CEO of Beacon Media + Marketing
and Beacon Digital University

BEACON
publishing + design

Published by Beacon Publishing & Design, 09/2024

ISBN 978-0-9831644-8-7 (Paperback)

ISBN 978-0-9831644-9-4 (Hardback)

ISBN 979-8-9915039-0-7 (Kindle)

1st edition September 2024

Printed in the United States of America

Library of Congress Control Number: 2024919761

Dedication

To my father, Brian, who navigated the line between being my therapist and my dad with grace, wisdom, and a whole lot of dry humor. You've constantly challenged me to look at both sides of situations and to hold space for people by believing in them even if they can't yet. Without your belief in me, I wouldn't have the experience to write this book.

To my mother, Sue, the heart of our family, thank you for always holding down the fort and keeping the lights on at "Green Home Base." Without your constant encouragement and deeply perceptive questions, I would not be the leader I am today.

To Jennifer, my co-founder and best friend, what a joy it has been to learn the ins and outs of marketing and business with you. Who would have thought…two girls from Alaska—but here we are, and we're just getting started.

To my husband, Bill, thank you for always believing in me and always being up for a new adventure! Without your love, encouragement, and making sure the ranch doesn't burn down while I'm distracted by work, this book and so many other insane ideas would have never had a chance to succeed and thrive.

To my son, Aidan, who constantly amazes me with his creativity and love of life. I love how much you care about people and your love of nu-metal music.

Intro

The emergence of the internet and social media have forever changed the face of marketing and advertising. The first significant shift started with the emergence of the internet, but it didn't gain momentum until the 2000s when the first smartphones enabled us to have a computer in our back pocket or purse. Suddenly, we were untethered from sitting in front of a computer, and the stage for a whole new age of marketing was set. It wasn't long before social media took advantage of these tiny computers, and marketing underwent another dynamic shift.

Digital marketing was born out of these turbulent times, and the chaos has only increased since. But amid the noise, some silver linings could be seen. The face of marketing had forever changed, and many of those changes flattened the playing field for mental health clinics, large and small. The internet and social media could now provide direct access to clients again. The middlemen of TV, radio, and big agencies weren't necessary anymore.

The most significant change in marketing and advertising was the transfer of influence from large corporations dictating consumer choices (outbound marketing) to consumers reclaiming their voice to express their preferences (inbound marketing). This shift from businesses interrupting consumers' lives to educating them about products and services they are interested in was particularly beneficial for mental health marketing.

Sadly, this monumental shift back to the customer has been diluted in recent years, and we are seeing a resurgance of ads interrupting our streaming movies, music, app experiences, and more. The consumer is no more happy about it now than I imagine we were when commercials first appeared in early TV and radio programs.

Undoubtedly, digital marketing is evolving at the speed of technology, and AI is bringing a new "age of intelligence." In these turbulent times, it is easy to get overwhelmed with the speed of change, new technologies, new terminology, and the constant changes of companies like Google and Meta as they try to adapt and react to the never-ending shifts.

So the question that continues to emerge is, where do I start? How do I market my mental health practice? Who do I trust to give me the correct information when everyone seems to be screaming for my attention?

I love these questions, and we will explore them and many others throughout this book. The summary of the answers is that fundamental marketing principles still apply no matter what technology you are using or what services your clinic specializes in. When you understand these principles, you can understand which tools will work best for your practice. The more complex things get, the more critical it is to return to the basics and keep it simple.

This book is for clinicians just starting out, small—to medium-sized clinics, and people in the mental or behavioral health industry interested in understanding marketing fundamentals. I hope you can use this book's straightforward nature to get your marketing up and running quickly and understand the marketing language and principles to better communicate with others in the field.

There is a lot of repetition in the different sections of this book and that is by intent. My hope is that this text can be as much of a reference tool allowing you to jump right to the section you need to know more about and have enough context and information in that section as you need to get questions answered and execute. So please feel free to read this book front to back or jump around to get the information most relevant to you right now!

Let's get started!

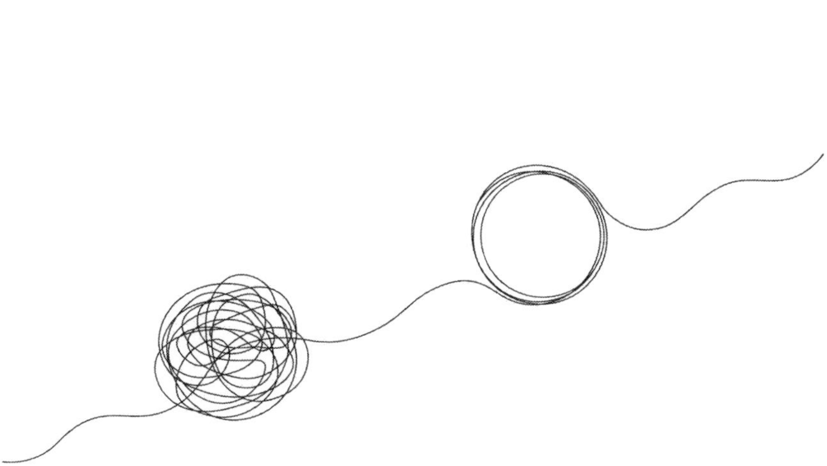

CHAPTER 1: Know Why You're Marketing

Understanding why you're putting the effort into marketing in the first place might sound like an overly simple statement, but hear me out. Marketing isn't just about getting more clients; while we all want and need more clients, there is more nuance to marketing. Clinics and practices market for a variety of reasons, including:

- Expanding market share in a specific geography or specialty (you're looking to get the majority of the clients out there who need you)
- Launching or relaunching a new specialty
- Increasing awareness of your clinic (your brand) or to build brand credibility
- Attract and retain top talent
- Generate potential partnerships or investors
- Get more clients

You're more than likely sharing the marketplace with competitors. They have their clients, and you have yours. You each have a percentage of the total revenue generated by people in a region. This is usually determined by taking the total revenue you are making and dividing it by the revenue generated for the whole industry.

For small businesses, this usually means how many local customers are booking appointments with you vs. another clinic or practitioner. Marketing increases awareness of your clinic and puts you in a position to increase the number of potential clients who are coming to you instead of a different provider.

Launching a New Service Line

Marketing around a new service or product can involve getting people to come to an open house or building excitement about providing a service that the market has been asking about and needing.

Increasing Brand Awareness and Credibility

Your brand is what people think of you when they hear the name of your clinic or practice. If your reputation is tarnished or no one has heard of you, you lack brand credibility, and people are less likely to book with you even if they like the types of specialties you're focusing on. It is essential to understand what people in the market think about your clinic and how you are coming across.

Building a solid brand through marketing is not just about awareness but also about loyalty. Strong brand loyalty is compelling for practices large and small. Think about brands like Apple, Toyota, Disney, Hilton, or Pizza Hut. People tend to be intensely loyal when they have benefited from the help you and/or your providers can deliver. Most people will want to share their story with others and can be dynamic referral sources.

Granted, not everyone can be Pizza Hut, but think about your local market. Marketing and commitments to quality, customer service, and your local community could make you the most loved place to get quality help. Branding is about knowing and owning who you are as a clinic or practice.

Attract and Retain Top Talent

It's common for people not to associate marketing with hiring and retaining quality practitioners or staff, but they go hand in hand. Your marketing is a powerful tool to increase awareness about your clinic culture, your fantastic team, and how you all work together. Good marketing with an eye for highlighting your people will help attract the right people who want to join that culture and dissuade people who may not be a good fit for your practice.

When your marketing is transparent, and people know who you are and what you stand for, they will know whether they want to align with that vision. Imagine having people come to you who want to work for you instead of always having to recruit.

Generate Potential Partnerships or Investors

Marketing means that people know about your practice, and they know what you are for and against. They know your story. It means you aren't the best-kept secret in town. This awareness increases opportunities for partnerships with others who could complement you.

Niching down to what you do best is another essential business principle, but it is scary for many clinics or practitioners for obvious reasons. These worries tend to center around being unable to provide a complete suite of services and losing clients to other clinics that will. Partnerships with other niche practitioners allow everyone to do what they do best and provide the best care for their clients!

Building a strong marketing presence can attract the right investors and positively affect your clinic's valuation if you're looking to grow your practice through investors or sell at some point.

Increase Clients

And here we are, folks. I saved the best for last. Yes, marketing is about increasing revenue! Marketing keeps potential clients coming to you. If you have a team that helps book clients, marketing keeps new leads coming to you.

A very important sidebar I want to highlight is that you want to ensure you have the infrastructure to handle new clients. A huge mistake we have seen often enough is when a clinic or practice launches their marketing campaign or hires an agency to launch their campaign, and suddenly, they are swamped with new leads and new clients. This sounds like a good thing, and it is an excellent problem to have, no doubt. But if you don't have a plan to handle the growth, you could end up overwhelming your team or your clinicians' capacity, and then you will lose clients.

Onboarding new clients is a reality but is almost always more costly than maintaining the ones you have. So before you start marketing heavily, make sure you can scale your company alongside your marketing and take care of your existing clients and those coming in. The last thing you want to do is torpedo your outstanding and hard-earned marketing efforts with bad revenue and lost clients because your company can't scale fast enough.

One element unique to mental health is that the goal should be to work your clients out of needing you. Most industries work to keep their clients for as long as possible, but with mental and behavioral health, the goal is to help them heal and move on with healthy lives. So, the specific lifespan of the clients must be kept in mind. Some clients might need help longer than others, but they all hopefully have a finite period as your client. Therefore, it is even more important to keep in mind that your marketing is essential to keep awareness high in your potential clients so that when they need you, they know where to find you.

Know Your Story

Now that you understand your reason for marketing let's spend some time understanding your story, which will lead you to your clinic's brand. A cohesive brand affects the marketplace and the clients it is trying to reach. A practice that lacks a strong, unified brand will be at the whim of the market and in danger of becoming fractured and anemic.

> *Your brand is how your business is perceived and the elements that create that perception.*

I'm not sure who first said the above quote, but it is one of the most to-the-point branding definitions I've heard. Many practice owners believe their brand is limited to their logo, so they stop there. A brand is so much more and a potent tool, so it is worth investing the time to get it right.

An effective brand consists of several elements, including:

- Your Story
- Your Values
- Your Promise
- Your Positioning
- Your Targeting
- Your Personality
- Your Visual Elements

Your origin story is, in many ways, the starting point for your whole brand. Why did you start your clinic? Who were you trying to help? What problem were you trying to solve for people? This is your Why (check out Simon Sinek's book *Start with Why* to dig deeper into or discover your why) and the foundation for your brand. People want to buy from people they know, like, and trust, and effectively communicating your story and your why goes a long way to establishing that connection with people. This concept is universal in business but ultimately crucial in mental and behavioral health. The level of vulnerability needed to see a therapist required a deeper level of trust to book an appointment.

The same could be said of people who want to work with you. They want to work (and you want to work) with people you all know, like, and trust. So start with your story and why when building your brand.

Your values naturally emerge from your story and your why. These are the guiding principles your clinic lives by, and they evaluate every decision made from the bottom to the top and back down. Keep them short, authentic, and genuine! They need to reflect and define the heart of your practice, not someone else's. Your values let the world know what you are against and what you are for.

Your promise is the one thing you commit to doing every time your clients interact with your clinic. Your brand promise connects to how your clients feel, which is vital because 80% of the time, clients make decisions based on their emotions. Your brand promise is another part of connecting to the marketplace, to the people who potentially want to see you or your clinicians or work for you.

A brand promise should never be a slogan or your unique selling position. Instead, it should go deeper. Your brand promise should set expectations for your clients and employees about their experiences with your practice, not about a specific service. It should be short and concise instead of short, catchy, and gimmicky, like taglines often are.

Your positioning as a brand is all about how you differ in your marketplace. What makes you different than other practices your potential clients could choose to see? You need to answer the question of why they should choose you. A great book that talks about market differentiation and how to choose the best marketplace to compete in is *Blue Ocean Strategy* by W. Chan Kim and Renee Mauborgne. To answer this question, you can do some research using competitors' websites, check out business research sites like Dun & Bradstreet, and narrow down your niche by specializing in a specific service, type of treatment, product, age democratic, or location.

According to Market Research (https://bit.ly/3TnX9lR), there are several specific areas you can focus on to differentiate yourself in the big world of business:

- Product or Service Offerings
- Distribution (who you take care of)
- Relationship
- Reputation
- Price

Your targeting is all about who your client is. One of the most significant traps practices fall into is thinking they must cast a wide net and try to connect with everyone. This is the opposite of the truth. The reality is that the more specific you are about your ideal client, the more effective your marketing and client retention will be. In the next chapter, we will discuss how to identify and understand your clients and how to connect with them through marketing.

Your personality or tone describes the manner in which you connect with your clients.

- Is your tone friendly and light-hearted? - Is it cheeky and irreverent?
- It is precise and very linear?
- Do you only work with high-level executives? Then, your tone needs to connect with them.

There isn't a right or wrong here; there is only what will resonate with your target market and brand. Both are vital! You need to ensure that the words and visual elements you use both resonate with your target market and are true to who your clinic is. If the tone that resonates with your target market doesn't also resonate with you, then you need to reevaluate. You need to shift your service to one that connects with your clinic and the people you want to help and are most qualified to work with. A disconnect here is severe and will lead to many significant problems. Avoid that kind of headache and lost revenue now, and make sure your marketing tone and values align with the clients you're trying to reach.

Your identity relates to all of the visual elements of your brand. These include but aren't limited to:

- Name
- Logo and the symbols or logo elements that complement it
- Company taglines and any campaign or advertising slogans
- Company colors
- Fonts and typography
- Additional visual elements

The **name of the company** might sound obvious, but nailing the name of your business is critical. It is common to name a company after a founder, which isn't necessarily bad, but it can limit the growth of the practice if the founder retires or sells the clinic and they are the face of it. This is also somewhat true of practices named after specific geographical names. Depending on the practice's growth, they can be limiting if the business wants to grow beyond the area they are named after.

Names that include some of what your clinic does or are named after a general but recognizable item have more longevity and equity. Some behemoth brands such as Goldman Sachs, Johnson & Johnson, Abercrombie & Fitch, and Ben and Jerry's Ice Cream have broken this rule. So it does and can happen, but the general rule of thumb is to stay away from naming something after yourself or to get creative with it like Bulgari (Italianized version of the family name of company founder Sotirios Voulgaris) or Audi (August Horch, audi is Latin for horch which means listen in English).

The **logo** and the symbols or icon elements that complement it are the core of any brand and the most recognizable. This is what many business owners think of when they hear brand. There are many iconic logos to get inspiration from, but remember that your logo should be timeless, clean, easily recognizable, and memorable. It is always worth investing in a quality graphic designer to put this together for you instead of trying to go with budget options like images from Word. A logo can be just an image like the iconic Apple or your company name, such as Coke or Coca-Cola. It can also be a combination of both, like Nike with both the name and the swoosh.

Company taglines and any campaign or advertising slogans are also part of your clinic's identity and should be noted as two different things. Your company tagline is timeless and doesn't change with various products or services. A slogan is specific to a campaign that focuses on a product or service. It will usually only last as long as the campaign, product, or service line.

Company colors must be chosen with the target market and your clinic's personality in mind. There is a world of information about how color affects us and what emotions it brings out in us. Check out this Shutterstock article for some examples: https://bit.ly/4gmUlzs. Again, working with a professional who understands how to use colors to connect with your target market and how to create a family of them for your practice's varied uses is an investment that cannot be minimized.

The **fonts** you use for your logo and other marketing materials do matter. You need to ensure the font reflects your practice's personality (light-hearted, educated, casual, formal, modern, traditional, etc.) and resonates with the clients you're connecting with.

One crucial point to consider is any copyright issues surrounding a font you chose to use. Some fonts are copyrighted by the original artist, and you must purchase the right to use them. There are also other resources below that include fonts that are open source, free to use, or have simple licensing. A professional designer should make sure they use fonts that either they have the right to use or they will advise you on purchasing those rights. Google Fonts is highly recommended because its fonts are more likely to translate into different browsers on your website.

- Fontesk: https://fontesk.com/license/free-for-commercial-use/
- Font Space: https://www.fontspace.com/commercial-fonts
- Google Fonts: https://fonts.google.com/

Additional visual elements could include using various elements from nature, your logo, or other places to compliment your overall brand and add visual interest to your marketing and other business materials. These might include mountains if your company has a connection to adventure or the outdoors and waves if your practice has any connection to the ocean or lakes. If you have an animal for your logo or your business mascot, you could even use the footprints of that animal as a visual element.

Other examples include natural shapes, such as flowers, leaves, and grass, or even geometric shapes, such as circles, triangles, and hexagons. Anything that enhances your core logo brings in visual contrast and interest.

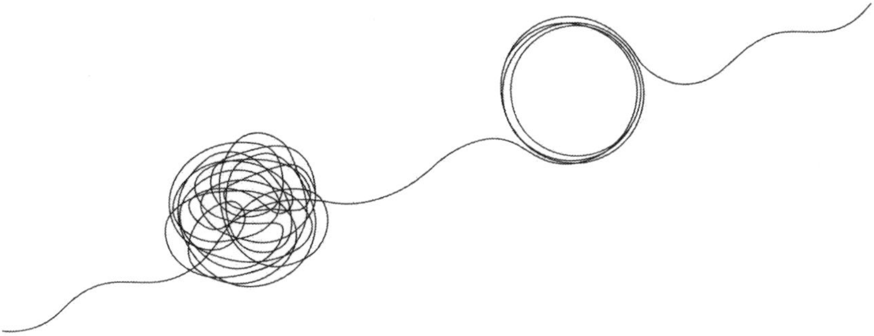

CHAPTER 2: Know Your Target Audience

Once you understand your why, the next step is to determine who you are trying to reach with your marketing. It's pretty common for clients to tell us that everyone is their client, but everyone is no one. If you try to market to everyone, you'll run into several serious problems.

The first problem with casting a wide net in your marketing is that your message becomes so generic that it won't appeal to anyone. Remember that you are marketing to people who don't like to be sold, but they will book with people they know, like, and trust. You have to connect with your audience, and the truth is that we don't connect with all people all the time.

People are looking for a message, a story they can see themselves in—and a generic story, isn't it. You must be specific and transparent with your marketing so people can relate to your practice and practitioners.

Another area for improvement with indistinct marketing is the cost. The broader the marketing, the more expensive it will be. The more specific your marketing, the more likely you are to attract the right client and not spend money on people who aren't your clients.

The first step in narrowing down your target audience is to segment and analyze your existing clients. Look through your current client list and identify the top 20% that bring in 80% of your revenue. This 80/20 rule is also called the Pareto principle and consistently holds true. Once you've roughly figured out your 20%, decide which ones you enjoy working with the most. Which of those 20% would you take on as a client if money were no object? These are your ideal clients.

Look through your current client list and identify the top 20% that bring in 80% of your revenue. This 80/20 rule, also called the Pareto principle, consistently holds true.

Once you've narrowed that down, the next step is to look for common themes between these remaining clients. Yes, you are profiling them, and this is where we need to touch on HIPAA and personal information. Make sure the personal information you are collecting and potentially sharing with a marketing agency or professional is stripped of any connection to the original person. You want to identify the type of person you can work best with, not expose someone's personal information.

Here are some questions you can answer about them (you might have to bring in staff who work with them directly for this part).

Biography: This part includes basic information about your ideal client, including age, gender, geographical information, ethnicity, name, occupation, marital status, etc.

Personal interests: In this section, it is time to discuss your buyer's personal interests in more detail, such as their hobbies and what they like to do when they aren't getting help from your clinicians. Even personal questions are essential to answer later when you start building your marketing because you are marketing to real people, not just families of people. The more authentic, personal, and transparent your marketing can be, the more effective it will be.

Goals: List several of your client's goals, including personal and professional ones.

Behavioral Traits: List out as many of their behavioral habits as you can, including what social media they use, how they get their information, what influences their decisions about who they trust, etc.

Challenges: Document their pain points, especially which pain points your clinic can address.

Objections: What could their objections be to booking with your facility?

Communication styles: Client communication styles refer to the different ways your clients prefer to interact and exchange information with you and your therapists. Understanding these styles can help tailor your marketing strategies to better meet patient needs and expectations. Here are some common client communication styles:

Assertive:

- Characteristics: Direct, clear, and confident.
- Preferences: Prefers straightforward and concise information. Values efficiency and quick resolution of issues.
- Best Approach: Be direct and to the point. Provide clear, actionable information without unnecessary details.

Analytical:

- Characteristics: Detail-oriented, logical, and methodical.
- Preferences: Prefers detailed explanations and data-driven information. Values thoroughness and accuracy.

- Best Approach: Provide comprehensive information with supporting data. Be prepared to answer detailed questions and offer step-by-step solutions.

Amiable:

- Characteristics: Friendly, cooperative, and relationship-focused.
- Preferences: Prefers a personal touch and building rapport. Values empathy and understanding.
- Best Approach: Be warm and friendly. Show genuine interest in their concerns and build a personal connection.

Expressive:

- Characteristics: Enthusiastic, creative, and outgoing.
- Preferences: Prefers engaging and dynamic interactions. Values innovation and new ideas.
- Best Approach: Use an enthusiastic and engaging tone. Highlight the benefits and innovative aspects of your solutions.

Driver:

- Characteristics: Goal-oriented, decisive, and results-focused.
- Preferences: Prefers quick and efficient communication. Values getting things done quickly.
- Best Approach: Be concise and focused on outcomes. Provide clear action plans and timelines.

Passive:

- Characteristics: Reserved, cautious, and non-confrontational.
- Preferences: Prefers gentle and non-threatening communication. Values reassurance and support.

- Best Approach: Be patient and reassuring. Provide clear guidance and support without overwhelming them.

Pragmatic:

- Characteristics: Practical, realistic, and solution-oriented.
- Preferences: Prefers practical solutions and tangible results. Values efficiency and effectiveness.
- Best Approach: Focus on practical solutions and tangible benefits. Provide clear steps and actionable advice.

Understanding and adapting to these different communication styles can significantly improve client satisfaction and loyalty. By tailoring your approach to match your client's preferred style, you can create more effective and meaningful interactions.

As you gather all this information, you can assemble your buyer personas to identify your target market. This will guide so much of everything else in this book. It will help you determine which channels to publish social media content on, the buyer journey through your website, the tone of your blogs, and maybe even the colors on your website.

There are various ways to collect data on potential buyers, especially if you're just getting started; you may not have enough of your ideal clients to go deep enough. Or, if you're launching a new product or service line, you might not have any profiles to start with. In that case, here are some additional ways to collect the data you need:

- Run qualitative (e.g., interviews) and quantitative (e.g., surveys) research
- Use customer feedback from reviews and customer support requests
- Communicate with your customer-facing teams
- Leverage analytics tools (e.g., Google Analytics and your CRM)

Use one of our templates to document the personas you've created, or grab one online. The key is to keep them as consistent as possible. Make sure to share your personas across the entire organization and keep them in an easily accessible place. Your buyer personas should be an active tool your team references regularly. Always observe and update your personas when needed. This often means regular client surveys and interviews to ensure you are still connecting with the right clients in the right way.

Resources for Buyer Persona Creation

- Miro: https://miro.com/templates/buyer-persona/
- Hubspot: https://offers.hubspot.com/persona-templates
- Canva: https://www.canva.com/templates/s/user-persona/
- SEMRush https://www.semrush.com/persona/
- Uxpressia https://uxpressia.com/ai-persona-generator

Understand the Buyer Journey

Understanding the buyer journey is much easier once you have your buyer personas built out. The buyer journey is the steps people go through before they actually book an appointment with you. Remember, in many ways, these steps are similar to how humans have always done things. The difference is that we do it digitally now instead of in person.

A recent LinkedIn study and a separate Hubspot study found that 98% of people will look up a local company online before deciding who to buy from. This startling statistic is made even more so by that small word…**local**. As marketers, we have seen stats like this for a while, but they were more commonly associated with regional or national brands. It is only recently that we've seen a percentage like this associated with local and regional facilities, clinics, or practices.

This makes it even more vital to understand the stages people commonly go through before you build out your marketing plan. The stages of the buyer's journey vary a bit online, but the most common are:

- Awareness (I think I might have a problem)
- Interest or Consideration (I think you might have a solution to my problem)
- Decision (You definitely have the solution I want, and I'm ready to book an appointment)

Let's dig into each stage, which questions to ask, and actions to take at each stage. Understanding clients' motivations at each stage of the buyer's journey means you can tailor your marketing and sales strategies to provide the correct information, support, and guidance to help clients move smoothly through the decision-making process. Knowing the right questions to ask at each stage of the buyer's journey means you can better understand the buyer's needs and preferences, address any concerns or objections they may have, and guide them toward making a decision that meets their needs. Understanding which targeted actions to take at each stage of the buyer's journey means you can effectively guide clients through the decision-making process and ultimately convert them into satisfied clients. These actions help build trust, provide value, and demonstrate the benefits of your services, leading to a successful and long-term relationship between your practice and your clients.

Awareness stage:

During the awareness stage, the client is in the process of discovering their problem or need. Often, they experience or identify symptoms of their problem but have not yet determined the root cause. Clients in this stage seek information and education to understand their situation better.

Their motivations at the Awareness Stage include:

- Identifying and understanding their challenge or need
- Exploring potential solutions and options available
- Researching and gathering information to make an informed decision
- Seeking to learn more about the industry, trends, and best practices

Questions specific to the Awareness Stage:

These questions can be asked by a booking service, a chatbot on your website, or even addressed by blogs on your website and social media posts.

- What challenges or issues are you currently facing? You will know the generic answer to this question from your prior research, so you can ask and answer it in blogs and address it in social media posts and paid ads. If you're using a chatbot or your appointment booking service is involved, they must ask this question.
- How did you become aware of our product/service?
- What are you looking for in a solution?
- Have you considered other options?

Actions specific to the Awareness Stage:

This stage is about gathering information. Most people are not ready to book an appointment when they are here. They are still trying to identify the problem they are trying to solve. With that in mind, focus on creating and publishing the following:

- Create educational content such as blog posts, articles, videos, or infographics to help customers understand their challenges and needs.
- Use targeted advertising and SEO strategies to reach clients searching for information about their challenges. Ensure

the targeted social posts, ads, or SEO content is informational and not pushy.

- Offer free resources or tools to help customers learn more about their challenges and potential solutions.
- Encourage customers to sign up for an email newsletter or follow social media channels to stay informed about industry trends and best practices.

Consideration Stage:

In the consideration stage, customers have clearly defined their challenge, need, or pain point and are actively weighing different solutions. Your potential clients compare different providers, consider the pros and cons, and determine which solution best fits their needs. They are deciding who to trust and who they connect with.

Their motivations at the Consideration Stage include:

- Evaluating different providers and clinics
- Comparing features, benefits, insurance, and pricing of different clinics
- Assessing how each provider aligns with their specific needs and goals
- Seeking recommendations, reviews, and testimonials from other clients

Questions for the Consideration Stage:

At this stage, an actual person should ask the questions. This could be a dedicated booking service or whoever in your company or organization is responsible for bringing in new clients.

- What specific features or benefits are you looking for in a solution?

- How do our providers compare to other options you are considering?
- What are your main criteria for making a decision?
- Do you have any concerns or objections about our providers or facility?

Actions for the Consideration Stage:

You can start being more specific in your language. People are looking for more details at this stage but aren't usually ready to book. In some ways, this is the trickiest stage because it is still about information gathering and comparing pros and cons. However, they usually aren't ready to decide, so if you push too hard here, they are more likely to choose a different provider.

- Provide detailed information, case studies, and testimonials to help clients evaluate solutions.
- Use email marketing and retargeting ads to stay engaged with potential clients who have visited your website or signed up for your email list and remind them of your facility's benefits.
- Provide personalized recommendations or comparisons to help clients make informed decisions, such as a free introductory or group session.

Decision stage:

Clients have narrowed their options at the decision stage and are ready to book an appointment. They evaluate the final details, such as pricing, location, availability, and which insurances are accepted, and often seek reassurance that they are making the right choice.

Their motivations at the Decision Stage include:

- Finalizing the decision-making process
- Negotiating terms and conditions and asking questions like:

    - Do you take my insurance?
    - Do you bill?
    - Do I have to pay upfront and seek reimbursement?
    - How soon can I be seen?
- Addressing any last-minute concerns or objections
- Seeking validation and confidence in their decision

Questions for the Decision Stage:

This is the time to book the appointment, so the questions should be very targeted and focused.

- What factors are most important to you when making a decision?
- What are the next steps in your decision-making process?
- Are any specific terms or conditions vital to you in the purchasing process?
- How soon do you need to make a decision?

Actions for the Decision Stage:

Now is the time to get the new client booked with your facility! Transparency is critical during this final stage regarding pricing, scheduling, insurance, etc.

- Offer special promotions or incentives to encourage clients to book an appointment.
- Provide transparent pricing and clear terms and conditions to help customers feel confident in their decisions.
- Offer a free consultation or demo to address any final concerns or objections.

CHAPTER 3: The HUB of Your Marketing

Today's marketing should be thought about like a wheel with spokes and a hub. Without the hub, the spokes don't go anywhere, and without the spokes, the hub is nice, but it doesn't get us anywhere fast.

The wheel's spokes are your various marketing tools: content marketing, social media, paid ads or PPC (pay-per-click), video marketing, and grassroots marketing. The central hub from which all the spokes come is your website! All the spokes (tools) should drive traffic to your website. It should never be just a pretty brochure online; it needs to be an active part of your marketing strategy.

Why should all of your marketing efforts drive traffic to your website?

All marketing efforts aim to get people to take action, whether to learn more about your clinic, book an appointment, attend an event, or sign up for your email list. To achieve these goals, we can use a variety of marketing channels, from paid advertising to social media to blogging to email. But no matter the channel, you must remember that all marketing efforts should drive traffic to your website.

Your website is the center of your marketing. It's the one place where you have complete control over your message and brand and where you can create the exact experience you want your potential clients to have. By driving traffic to your website, you can engage your audience, provide valuable information, and ultimately turn them into leads and clients.

Your website should not be an online brochure but a tool that generates leads and revenue.

Your website is a prime opportunity to establish your company and your facility as a credible and trustworthy brand. When visitors arrive at a well-designed, informative, and user-friendly website, they are more likely to view your practice as one they can trust. This, in turn, can lead to long-term client loyalty and increased conversions.

This starts by positioning your website as the go-to resource for industry expertise, providing valuable content that demonstrates your authority and increases conversions. To do this, you have to move beyond basic service descriptions by highlighting the unique ways your providers and facility help and address standard client concerns. You can position your brand/facility as the best solution for your clients' challenges. You can build a connection and help your potential patients feel welcomed and safe.

In the next chapter, we will explore what makes an effective website because your website is one of your most important marketing assets. You cannot create it once and then leave it alone for years. Those days have come and gone. And I get it; websites can be daunting. It can be hard to wrap your brain around what they can do for you. But it is time we think about websites as a place where you can build your brand, attract new visitors, generate leads, and nurture relationships of trust with your clients. But to do that, you must create a user-friendly, informative, and engaging website that is constantly evolving and growing with you and your clients.

Putting up a fantastic website doesn't ensure people will find it. This is not like a *Field of Dreams* [film] where "build it, and they will come" works. A well-built website will eventually get you traffic, but you must leverage your marketing tools to ensure it is the powerhouse it can be. Let's take a 10,000-foot view of how your marketing tools (spokes) engage with your website (the hub) and help it all come together faster.

Evergreen Content & Email content

Evergreen content refers to timeless, relevant information that remains valuable and useful to readers over an extended period, regardless of when it was published. This type of content is not

> *Evergreen content refers to timeless, relevant information that remains valuable and useful to readers, regardless of when it was published.*

tied to current events or trends, making it a reliable resource that continues to attract and engage audiences long after its creation. Evergreen content offers potential clients helpful information and can be a resource for lead generation and revenue. By crafting consistently relevant and interesting material for your audience (answering their questions), you can keep visitors on your site longer and encourage them to return.

Once you've crafted your evergreen content, don't let it gather dust. Regular updates keep it relevant. Freshen it up with the latest info and stats and ensure all links work. Then, spread the word on social media and other platforms to extend its reach and impact.

Your evergreen content, along with announcements about current offerings, events, specials, new providers, and other helpful information, are the perfect subjects for email marketing. Email marketing is about keeping your brand at the forefront of clients' minds and driving traffic back to your website to take action.

Paid Ads or PPC

Paid advertising is an effective tool for directing targeted traffic to your website. By leveraging platforms such as Google Ads, social media advertising, and native advertising (material in an online publication that resembles the publication's editorial content but is paid for by an advertiser and intended to promote the advertiser's product), you can reach individuals interested in your offerings and motivate them to explore your website.

Paid advertising is a potent ally in your quest for business growth. When used well, it can significantly boost your website traffic, translating to more leads, clients, and revenue. The key is to target your ads to the right audience and have those ads targeted to the correct pages on your website. When people click on an ad, they expect to be taken to a page on your website that addresses the subject matter in the ad. If the ad takes them to a different page, the home page, or a contact page, they will be frustrated, and they are more likely to bounce or leave your site as fast as they came. Make sure an ad about a specific service or product takes them directly to that page on your website, not something general.

Social Media Content

In our digital age, social media platforms are a potent means for your business to engage with its audience and direct traffic to your website. With billions of active users, social media presents an unparalleled opportunity to connect with potential clients and bolster brand recognition. When you create and share content that connects with your audience, potential clients are more likely to interact on social media and visit your websites to learn more. Moreover, the strategic promotion of website information, such as new blog posts, new providers, or special offers, across social media platforms can serve as an added incentive for users to explore your website and its offerings.

Additionally, social media is a powerful tool for spotlighting your practice's culture and job opportunities. You can offer a peek behind the curtain, highlight your team, and share open positions; you can forge connections with your audience and draw in potential employees who are aligned with your company's vision. This approach bolsters your brand and entices qualified individuals to your website, where they can learn more and apply for available roles.

Posting regularly on social media platforms offers a direct conduit to potential clients. It allows us to interact, provide valuable insights, and turn visitors into loyal clients.

Video Content

Video content is a powerful tool to engage your audience, increase conversions, and build brand loyalty. There are a variety of types of videos that are effective, including:

- **Service videos** are a dynamic way to present your service specialties, demonstrating their features and benefits in action.
- **Tutorial and educational videos** can be game-changers, offering your audience the solutions or skills they seek. For

example, they could teach how to breathe through a panic attack or recognize the symptoms of being triggered. These videos also build trust and credibility and attract leads.

- **Video testimonials** demonstrate how your providers have positively impacted others and provide social proof, which is key in establishing trust and credibility. This one is more difficult in the mental and behavioral health space. But if you have clients brave enough to go on video, those will become some of the most powerful tools you have to connect with clients at a fundamental level.
- **Behind-the-scenes** videos can also be powerful when you show potential patients what they can expect to experience when they walk into your waiting area or what type of play therapy rooms you have. Considering the anxiety that often accompanies seeking help for mental health issues, helping them prepare for what they are going to experience walking in the door can set them at ease, thereby forging a deeper connection between your audience and your brand.
- **Company culture videos** are a great way to attract and retain top talent through brand awareness and loyalty. They also help potential patients understand on a deeper level what motivates you and your practitioners to do what they do.

Additional Marketing Tools

Additional marketing tools also help drive traffic to your site if used correctly. It is important to remember that the point of all your marketing is to drive traffic to your site so you can track it, analyze it, and improve on it. When your website is set up to be a dynamic conversion tool, it should always be the hub of even your offline marketing endeavors.

Here are some effective tactics and tools to consider:

- **Conferences & Trade Shows**: These are great ways to get your brand out to industry-specific crowds. Make sure you make it easy for people to find your website address on everything you give away at the conference.
- **Print Marketing**: Display your website address prominently on printed marketing materials, such as business cards, flyers, brochures, and company vehicles. Ensure that the URL is easily visible and that visitors understand what they will find on your site.
- **TV & Radio:** This is a challenging tool for directing website traffic because you only have a very short period of time to display or say your URL (website address). However, it is still vital to direct traffic to your site for tracking and conversion purposes.
- **Grassroots Marketing**: By actively participating in your local community and forging connections with potential clients, you can generate excitement around your business and motivate individuals to visit your site for further information.

The more tools you use to direct traffic to your website, the more likely you are to have more leads and, therefore, more opportunities to convert them to actual clients. But that doesn't mean you must leverage every tool above to be effective. Consistency and quality are more important than volume. Various factors can affect your marketing effectiveness, and it is vital to consider their pros and cons when building your marketing strategy.

Your Time: You only have so much time in a day, week, month, or year, and we all know there are always more demands on that time than we…well, have time for. Rather than start with everything you want to do and try to find the time for it (because you probably won't be able to), look at how much time you can realistically set aside for marketing and then fit the tools you use into that time. Put the time on your calendar like a meeting and treat it like the important meeting that it is. It's okay if all you can do is an hour or two a week to start. If that's what you have, then begin there.

Ideally, businesses spend 5-7% of revenue on marketing. If you are growing aggressively, plan on 10% of revenue

---

Your Financial Resources: Some marketing is more costly than others, and some take more time than money. Ideally, businesses spend 5-7% of their revenue on marketing; if they are growing aggressively, that number jumps to 10%. If your budget is more about time than money, organic social media posts, blogs you write, and grassroots marketing might be your best route. From there, you can add more tools that take financial resources as it works with your budget.

Skills: Let's face it, not all of us are great writers or comfortable in group networking situations. Try to align your skills with specific types of marketing. Sometimes, we all have to grit our teeth and do something we don't love to get a particular result. However, with the knowledge that consistency is vital in marketing, it helps to focus on what you or some of your staff are better at and enjoy.

Now that we have identified why we are marketing, we know why it is essential to know our customers, and we understand how all of the tools drive traffic to our website and lead to conversions; let's explore the individual tools before we pull it all together in the marketing strategy.

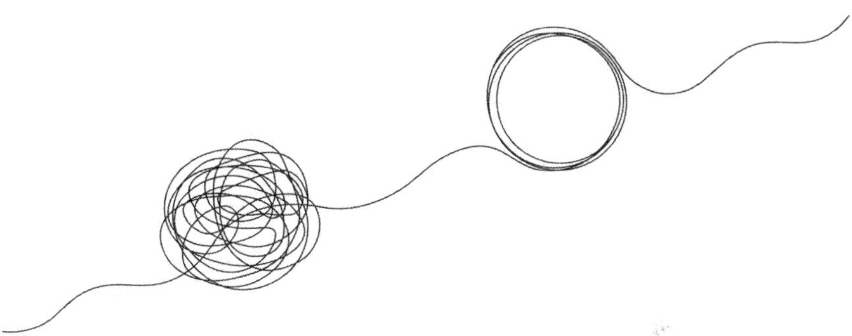

Chapter 4: What Makes a Good Website?

A good website is characterized by several key elements that attract visitors and convert them into clients or followers. Here are essential components that make a website stand out:

Effective Brand Representation: Your website should accurately reflect your brand's personality and values. This includes using visuals and language that align with your brand to create a consistent visitor experience. The design and layout (together referred to as the user interface or UI) should be inviting and resonate with your target audience, as this directly influences their perception of your brand.

User-Friendly Design: A crucial aspect of a good website is its user-friendly design. This design ensures an easy and intuitive user experience, with fast load times, mobile responsiveness, and easy navigation. By being accessible from various devices and providing quick and easy access to information, your website can prevent user frustration and confusion, reducing the likelihood of someone abandoning your site before you even get a chance to connect with them.

High-Quality Content: Another critical element of a good website is its high-quality content. This content should be engaging, informative, and relevant to your audience and include well-written text, high-quality images, and videos that enhance the user experience. Not only does this content need to be optimized for search engines to improve visibility and drive traffic, but it also needs to be compelling and valuable to the reader, driving user engagement and SEO.

Search Engine Optimization (SEO): A good website is optimized for search engines to increase visibility and attract more visitors. This involves using the right keywords, creating quality content, and ensuring your site has all the technical elements to rank well in search results.

Backlinks: These are incoming links from one website to another and play a significant role in SEO and can positively impact your website's visibility, authority, and overall online presence. They are crucial for SEO as they signal to search engines that other websites consider your content valuable and trustworthy. Backlinks are a vote of confidence in your website's content and can help improve its visibility and ranking in search engine results. However, backlinks from spammy, irrelevant, or low-quality websites can harm your website's SEO. Search engines may penalize your site for having unnatural or manipulative backlinks. So, using tools like SEMrush, Google Search Console, or Moz Pro with backlink audit tools is vital to determine toxic links that can hurt your SEO ranking.

Strong Calls to Action (CTAs): Effective CTAs guide your site's visitors toward taking a desired action, such as requesting more information, signing up for a newsletter, or scheduling an appointment. They should be clear, compelling, and strategically placed throughout your website to draw attention and encourage engagement.

Trustworthiness and Credibility: Client testimonials, case studies, reviews, and clear contact information help establish trust. Since your website is often your first chance to make a good impression, leveraging as many opportunities as you can truthfully use to build trust with potential customers is crucial. Other tools, including showcasing awards, certifications, and professional affiliations, can boost credibility. Once again, it goes without saying that all case studies should follow HIPAA regulations.

Regular Updates and Fresh Content: A good website must be updated with fresh content and the latest information about your products or services. This boosts your SEO and shows that your business is active and growing, which indicates to visitors that your company is up-to-date and trustworthy.

Security Features: Keeping your website secure is essential, particularly when handling sensitive customer information. SSL certificates, regular updates, and secure checkout options are vital to protecting your users and business.

Incorporating these elements will help create a website that looks good and performs well in terms of user engagement and conversion.

Website + Domain Ownership

Unfortunately, there are many agencies and website development firms out there with some shady practices that usually involve owning various parts (or all) of your website and domain name without your knowledge. When you use a third party to help you design your site (Wix or Squarespace, for example) or hire a freelancer or agency to design it for you, please, please, please verify that you will 100% own the website content, design, and domain name when the project is done, and you've made your last payment. You might have to read the fine print and ask your account manager for written confirmation, but make sure you get in writing what you do and do not own.

Your domain address is your URL such as www.beaconmm.com or www.forbes.com. This website address tells the search engine where to go to view your website. Your actual website design and information is sitting in the memory of a hosting service. When someone types in your URL or domain name, they are telling the search engine to go to that hosting service and access the website that is stored there. This is why is absolutely critical that you own both your domain name as well as the design and content of your website.

When you own everything and you want to move to a new hosting company, freelancer, or agency, the place you are leaving can transfer everything to the next hosting company or agency.

Effective Brand Representation

You never get a second chance to make a first impression, or so the saying goes. This is often true of your website, so effective brand representation is crucial because it sets the tone for how visitors perceive and interact with your brand, which reflects your clinic. A website that effectively embodies your brand will incorporate key elements reflecting its tone and values, creating a consistent and engaging visitor experience.

Visuals and Design: Your business's personality (brand) should be reflected in the choice of colors, fonts, imagery, and overall design aesthetics. For instance, a brand that wants to appear warm and inviting might use soft colors and friendly imagery. Your chosen visual elements should consistently echo your brand's identity across all pages. This consistency in visual design helps reinforce identity and can make the brand more memorable to visitors.

Language and Content: The language used on the website should mirror the brand's voice, whether it's professional, conversational, or technical. This extends to all written content, from homepage copy to detailed blog posts. The content should not only reflect the brand's values but should also be customized to the needs and interests of the target audience. For example, a brand that values transparency might include a detailed About Us page that shares the company's history, values, and people or comprehensive service descriptions that explain how they help a specific type of client get help and live a happy and pain-free life.

User Experience (UX): Your website's user interface should be designed with your target audience in mind, ensuring it is intuitive and easy to navigate for the visitor. A good UX design will make your potential customers feel at ease, helping them find information quickly and efficiently and enhancing their overall perception of the brand. This includes having a responsive design that works well on desktop and mobile devices and ensuring that interactive elements like buttons and links are easy to use and functional. As of February 2024, the vast majority of people use their mobile devices to access websites; in fact, the ratio is 4 to 1. However, desktop users visit more pages when they visit, stay longer, and have lower bounce rates.

Consistency: Across the website, consistency in design, language, and user experience reinforces the brand's message and values. This consistency helps build a strong brand image that visitors can easily recognize, which is crucial for establishing trust and credibility.

Engagement: Engaging with visitors through well-placed CTA's, interactive elements, and dynamic content can also reflect and enhance a brand's personality. For instance, a youthful and dynamic brand might use modern, interactive elements like animated transitions with a clean look and feel with a lot of white space. A clinic that works with children in crisis might use softer, warm colors that resonate with parents and communicate a safe and welcoming environment.

Effective brand representation on a website involves a careful blend of visual design, content, user interface, and overall consistency, all tailored to resonate with the target audience. This strategic alignment helps create a compelling digital presence that accurately reflects your brand's identity and values. This fosters a positive perception and relationship with your potential customers, thus increasing the likelihood they will buy from you instead of a competitor. Since you probably won't get a second chance to make a great first impression, ensure your website reflects your business well and connects with your target audience.

User-friendly Design

User-friendly design is a cornerstone of a successful website, as it directly influences how visitors interact with your site and, ultimately, their impression of your brand.

Fast Load Times: The speed at which your website loads is critical! Slow loading times can frustrate users and lead to higher bounce rates. Websites need to be optimized for speed by compressing images, leveraging browser caching, and minimizing the use of heavy scripts and plugins. The goal is to remove as many barriers as possible for your website visitors, so ensuring that your website functions quickly and efficiently is essential for a positive user experience.

Mobile Responsiveness: With the increasing use of mobile devices to access the internet, your website must perform well on smartphones and tablets. This means having a responsive design that adjusts the layout based on the device's screen size. Mobile responsiveness enhances usability by ensuring that text is readable, links and buttons are clickable, and navigation is smooth, regardless of the device used.

Easy Navigation: Navigation should be intuitive and straightforward. A well-organized menu that categorizes information logically helps users find what they need quickly. I can't emphasize enough the importance of clear navigation pathways, including a visible menu bar, a search function, and minimal clicks required to reach the desired content. This simplicity in design prevents users from feeling overwhelmed and helps guide them through your site more effectively.

Clear Menus and Minimal Pop-Ups: Users should be able to find essential information quickly. Clear, concise menus that are easy to understand play a critical role in enhancing user experience. Additionally, while pop-ups can be helpful for conversions, they should be used sparingly as they can be intrusive and negatively impact the user experience if overused.

Clean and Simple Layout: A clutter-free layout helps maintain the user's focus on important content. A clean design with adequate white space improves readability and visual appeal. Each page should be designed with a clear focus, and all elements should contribute towards the user's understanding and engagement.

Consistent Design Elements: Consistency in design across all pages reduces users' cognitive load and makes the interaction more predictable and easier to understand. This includes consistent use of colors, font styles, and layout patterns. Visual elements that are appealing and aligned with the brand are essential to enhance the overall user experience.

Incorporating these elements of user-friendly design improves the functionality and accessibility of your website. It enhances the overall satisfaction of your visitors, making them more likely to engage with your content, return to your site, and convert into customers.

High-Quality Content

High-quality content is not just important; it's pivotal! It's the key to engaging your audience and enhancing your website's online visibility. There are several layers to creating content that attract and retain user interest while being optimized for search engines.

Engaging and Informative Content: The primary goal of your website's content is to engage users and provide them with valuable information that addresses their needs and questions. This can be through detailed service descriptions, informative blog posts, or FAQs that directly answer standard queries. At Beacon Media + Marketing, we emphasize the importance of content that educates and informs, such as detailed explanations of services offered, which helps establish authority and trust with the audience.

Well-Written Text: Clarity and ease of reading are crucial. The text should be well-structured with headings, subheadings, and bullet points to break up text and make information easy to scan. I suggest using clear, concise language reflecting your brand's voice, enhancing readability and engagement. It is easy to get caught up in your industry's technical jargon and acronyms; we all do it. But the more you can use content that connects with your audience, the better, and that usually means removing the industry jargon and speaking from the heart.

High-Quality Images and Videos: Visual content can significantly enhance user engagement. High-quality images and videos should be aesthetically pleasing and relevant to the accompanying text. They break up content, illustrate points, and provide a richer user experience. Use infographics and quotes in a visually appealing way to summarize key points, thereby making complex information more accessible to digest and more engaging.

SEO Optimization: Content must be optimized for search engines to improve visibility and drive traffic. This involves organically using relevant keywords throughout the text, optimizing meta tags (snippets of text that describe a webpage's content but do not appear on it) and descriptions, and structuring content so search engines can easily understand. Content needs to be tailored to meet your target audience's specific needs, improving user experience and enhancing SEO efforts.

Regular Updates and Fresh Content: Keeping your content updated is not just important; it's vital for maintaining the relevance and freshness of your website. Regular updates signal to search engines that your site is active, helping to maintain or improve your search rankings. You must update service pages and blogs regularly to keep content current and relevant, encouraging repeat visits and boosting user engagement.

Value and Relevance: Every piece of content on your website should add value to your audience. This means providing them with the answers they seek, offering solutions to their problems, or sharing unique and beneficial knowledge.

Incorporating these elements into your website's content strategy will enhance the user experience and improve your site's SEO performance, leading to better visibility and higher engagement rates.

Strong Calls to Action (CTAs)

Strong Calls to Action (CTAs) are essential to effective website design and content strategy. CTAs serve as guides that lead users toward taking specific actions that align with the business's goals, such as making a purchase, signing up for a newsletter, or scheduling an appointment. Here's a deeper look into how effective CTAs can be crafted and implemented based on the insights provided:

Clarity and Compelling Language: CTAs should be straightforward and use action-oriented language that leaves no doubt about what the user is expected to do next. Phrases like "Download My Checklist," "Schedule A Call," or "Learn More" are direct and clear, effectively communicating the action the user is expected to take.

Strategic Placement: The placement of CTAs on a website is crucial for maximizing user engagement. They should be placed in high-visibility areas where users naturally focus, such as near the top of a page or in the central part of the content where they are more likely to draw attention. It is vital to use them both at the beginning and the end of areas of content, ensuring that users have multiple opportunities to engage with the call to action as they consume the content.

Design and Contrast: To make CTAs stand out, they should be designed with contrasting colors or features that differentiate them from the rest of the page. This can involve using bold buttons, highlighted text, or icons that draw the eye.

Relevance and Value: The CTAs should offer clear value to the user, making it evident what benefits they will gain by taking the action. Whether it's accessing a free resource, getting a personalized consultation, or learning more about a service, the CTA should align with the interests and needs of the target audience.

Frequency and Repetition: While it's important not to overwhelm the user with too many CTAs, strategically repeating them across the site can be effective. This ensures that engaged and interested users always have a clear next step to take without searching for it. Use CTA's at strategic points in your website, ensuring users are regularly prompted to take action as they move through the site.

By incorporating these elements, CTAs can significantly enhance the user experience on a website, guiding visitors toward conversion in an effective and user-friendly way.

Trustworthiness and Credibility

Trustworthiness and credibility are crucial elements that significantly influence a user's decision to engage with a business online, which can lead the user to convert from an interested party (a lead) to a new client.

Customer Testimonials and Case Studies: These are powerful tools for building trust and credibility. They provide real-life examples of former clients' satisfaction and successful outcomes, which help potential clients feel more confident in choosing your services. Prominently showcasing these elements on your website lets you communicate your services' direct benefits and reliability to prospective clients. Testimonials and case studies can only be done with former clients, and you cannot disclose any specific treatment or personal information.

Reviews: Similar to testimonials, reviews offer honest feedback from past clients and are highly valued by potential patients. They provide insight into the client experience and the quality of service offered. It's not just about responding to reviews, particularly negative ones, but doing so constructively and positively. This can further enhance trust by showing that your business values feedback and is committed to continuous improvement. Remember, when responding to reviews, you cannot acknowledge that the person who left the review is a client. You can thank them for the review and the feedback, but nothing more per HIPAA regulations.

Awards, Certifications, and Professional Affiliations: Displaying awards and certifications showcases your achievements and signals to users that industry leaders recognize and validate your business.

Professional Affiliations: Being part of professional organizations or industry groups can also boost credibility. It shows that your business and practitioners adhere to specific standards and practices valued by the industry, which can reassure clients of your professionalism and commitment to quality.

Incorporating these elements into your website is not just a suggestion but a strategic move that can significantly enhance the trustworthiness and credibility of your business. By transparently showcasing your successes, customer satisfaction, and industry recognition, you can build a stronger rapport with potential clients, encouraging them to engage confidently with your services.

SEO Optimization

SEO (search engine optimization) is critical to a successful digital marketing strategy. SEO involves enhancing various aspects of a website to improve its visibility and ranking on search engines like Google. This process is crucial for attracting more visitors to your site. Here are the critical components of SEO optimization as discussed in the sources:

- Using the Right Keywords
- Creating Quality Content
- Technical SEO Elements
- Regular Updates and Fresh Content
- Backlinks

SEO involves enhancing various aspects of a website to improve its visibility and ranking on search engines like Google.

By focusing on these aspects, SEO optimization makes your website more attractive to search engines and users, increasing traffic and potentially increasing conversions. Here's a deeper dive into the key aspects of SEO optimization based on insights from the sources:

Using the Right Keywords: Keywords are the cornerstone of SEO. They help search engines understand your website and match your content to what users are searching for. You need to use keyword research tools like [Google Keyword Planner] to identify the terms and phrases that potential customers use to find services or products like yours. This research not only informs the content you create but also helps in optimizing the metadata (Metadata is data that provides information about other data, such as the title, author, or date of creation of a document. It helps organize and describe information for easier search and retrieval) and URLs for better search engine rankings. (URL stands for Uniform Resource Locator. It is the address used to locate resources, such as websites or files, on the internet.)

Creating Quality Content: As we said earlier, the content on your website must be engaging, informative, and relevant to your audience. It must also be structured so that search engines can easily understand it. This includes using headers and subheaders and incorporating keywords naturally throughout the articles.

Technical SEO Elements: Another crucial aspect of SEO is ensuring that your website is technically optimized. This includes improving site speed, ensuring your website is mobile-friendly, and having a secure and accessible website. Technical SEO also involves using structured data to help search engines better understand your site's content and structure. This can include schema markup, which helps to classify and display your content in an appealing way in search results.

Regular Updates and Fresh Content: You'll notice I keep returning to this. Search engines favor websites that are regularly updated with fresh content, which signals to search engines that your website is active. Regular updates can involve adding new blog posts, updating existing articles and pages, or removing outdated content. This helps maintain or improve your search rankings and keeps your audience engaged.

Backlinks: Building a network of backlinks from reputable sites is another effective SEO strategy. Backlinks are links from other websites to your site, which search engines use as a signal of the credibility and authority of your content. Focus on quality over quantity by seeking backlinks from well-regarded sites within your industry, which can significantly boost your SEO performance.

Local SEO + Listing Services

Listing services, such as therapist directories like Psychology Today, are platforms where mental health professionals can list their services, making it easier for potential clients actively seeking help to find them.

Using listing services as part of your local SEO marketing offers significant benefits because it enhances your visibility to potential clients who are actively seeking therapy services. These services serve as a crucial entry point, making it easier for people to find and connect with mental health professionals in their area. Having current clinic information on these listing sites can lead to an increase in client inquiries and engagements, as the directory positions the company's services in front of a targeted audience looking for specific mental health support. Finally, being listed in reputable directories can also boost a company's credibility and professional image, further attracting clients and building trust within the community.

Some of the sites we currently recommend for mental health clinics to secure listings on are:

- Psychology Today (see this link for details on an effective listing https://bit.ly/3MQEZpd)
- Therapy for Black Girls
- Mental Health Match
- Therapy Den
- Therapy Tribe
- Your Google Business Profile (https://www.google.com/intl/en_us/business/)

Your listings are a significant part of your local SEO marketing, but there are also other items that are important to consider, including:

- **NAP Consistency**: Ensuring your Name, Address, and Phone number (NAP) are consistent across all online platforms and directories.
- **Local Keywords**: Use relevant local keywords in your descriptions to help search engines understand your location-specific relevance.

- **Online Reviews:** Encouraging and managing positive reviews on platforms like Google, Yelp, and Facebook, as they can impact your local search rankings.
- **Citations**: Building consistent citations (mentions of your business NAP) on authoritative local directories and websites.
- **Schema Markup**: Implementing schema markup to provide search engines with more detailed information about your business, such as hours of operation and reviews. If you're unfamiliar with what schema markup is, it is a specific type of structured data markup that is added to a website's HTML code to provide search engines with more context about the content on the page. It helps search engines better understand the content of a webpage, which can lead to higher rankings and increased visibility in search results. Your website team or marketing agency can help you implement this if it's not already on your site.
- **Local Link Building**: Acquiring backlinks from local news outlets, community organizations, and other relevant health-related websites
- **Google Maps Integration**: Embedding Google Maps on your website can help users find your business easily
- **Regular Updates**: Keeping your website and GBP listing updated with current information, such as business hours and contact details
- **Location-Specific Landing Pages**: If you have multiple physical locations, creating unique landing pages for each location can enhance local SEO

Check out this article on local SEO for more details https://bit.ly/4gslrVP

Website Security

Website security is important for many reasons, including protecting patients' sensitive and confidential information. A breach in website security could lead to unauthorized access to patient data, which can have serious consequences such as identity theft, breach of confidentiality, and reputational damage to the clinic. Ensuring website security helps maintain patient trust and demonstrates a commitment to safeguarding their privacy and information.

The following aspects of website security are great places to start:

- **Secure hosting**: Ensure the website is hosted on a secure server with encryption protocols to protect data transmission.
- **SSL certificate:** Install an SSL certificate to encrypt data transmitted between the website and users, providing a secure connection.
- **Regular updates:** Keep the website's software, plugins, and themes up to date to patch security vulnerabilities and protect against cyber threats.
- **Strong passwords**: Use strong, unique passwords for website admin accounts and encourage users to do the same to prevent unauthorized access.
- **Access control**: Use role-based access control to limit access to sensitive data and functionalities to authorized personnel only.
- **Regular backups**: Implement regular backups of website data to ensure that information can be restored in case of a security incident.
- **Malware protection**: Install security plugins or software to scan for malware and protect the website from malicious attacks.

- **Security monitoring:** Monitor website traffic, logs, and security alerts for any suspicious activity that could indicate a security breach.

By focusing on these critical areas of website security, you can better protect patient data and maintain the confidentiality and integrity of their online services.

Chatbots on Websites

Chatbots can enhance user engagement and provide personalized assistance to website visitors, improving their overall experience. They can respond immediately to frequently asked questions, support users in navigating the website, and guide them to relevant resources. By leveraging chatbots, websites can increase user satisfaction, streamline communication, and provide an efficient way to connect with potential clients.

Customer Service Enhancement: Chatbots significantly improve customer service by immediately responding to user inquiries. This instant interaction helps address customer concerns quickly, increasing satisfaction and loyalty. Tools like Talk Further can be customized to the needs of your mental or behavioral health clientele.

24/7 Availability: Chatbots offer around-the-clock service, allowing users to get answers to their questions at any time. This is especially beneficial for businesses that deal with customers in different time zones.

Handling Capacity: Chatbots can handle a large volume of queries simultaneously, reducing the workload on human customer service representatives and ensuring that user inquiries are not left unanswered.

Consistency in Responses: Chatbots consistently answer frequently asked questions, ensuring all users receive the same information. This consistency helps maintain your clinic's reliability and credibility.

User Engagement: Chatbots can enhance the user experience on the website by engaging users through interactive conversations. They keep users engaged by providing quick and interactive responses, which can lead to increased time spent on the site and potentially higher conversion rates.

Chatbots on websites can become a hotly debated topic. Some people love them, and some hate them, so we know they have pros and cons. We talked above about the many benefits; let's look at some downsides.

Cons of Having Chatbots on Your Website

Limited Response Capability: Chatbots are typically programmed to answer predefined questions and may need help with complex or unique customer queries that require human intuition and understanding. If users' questions are outside the scope of the chatbot's programming, this can sometimes lead to frustration.

Impersonal Interaction: While efficient, chatbots lack the personal touch that human interaction offers. They may be unable to manage nuanced emotional cues or provide the empathy that a human representative can.

Overdependence: Relying heavily on chatbots can lead to neglect in other areas of customer service, such as personal customer support and service customization. Maintaining a balance is critical to ensure that all customer needs are adequately met.

Technical Issues and Maintenance: Chatbots require regular updates and maintenance to function effectively. Technical glitches can impair their functionality, leading to poor user experiences if not promptly addressed.

If implemented thoughtfully, chatbots can significantly enhance operational efficiency and customer interaction. However, their limitations must be considered. Balancing automated interactions with human touchpoints is crucial to providing comprehensive customer service.

Primary Navigation Items

The top line of the website serves as the navigation and helps people find their way through the information and how it is sorted on your website. Don't get too creative with this, or people will get lost. Typically, it is on the upper right-hand side of the site above the main image. You can get very intricate with navigation bars and the sub-menus under them, but we encourage you to resist the urge and always try to keep it as simple as possible.

Here are the basics and often all you need in the navigation bar:

Home Page

Clear and concise messaging: At the heart of every great home page is clear and concise messaging. This may seem like a no-brainer, but you'd be surprised how many websites fail to communicate their value proposition effectively. Your home page is your chance to make a positive first impression and capture visitors' attention, so getting your messaging right is essential.

Start with a headline that grabs the reader's attention and clearly describes what your page is about. Think of it as the title of a great story that makes people want to keep reading. Follow it up with a subheading that provides more information about the headline and what the reader can expect to find on the page. This is your chance to expand on your value proposition and give visitors a reason to keep reading.

Remember that less is more when you write the body of your text. Keep your paragraphs brief and your language straightforward and accessible. Avoid jargon and technical terms that could alienate your audience. Use bullet points or lists to make your information easy to skim. The aim is to communicate your message clearly without overwhelming your visitors with too much text.

Prioritize clear and concise messaging. This is the foundation of a successful home page. It engages your visitors, communicates your values, provides a dynamic way to connect, and sets the stage for further website exploration.

Effective use of visuals. A great home page should feature large, high-quality images that reflect your brand and tell your story. When choosing images, make sure they are relevant, authentic, and visually appealing. Ideally, avoid generic stock photos and instead invest in custom photography that showcases your brand's personality, but if that isn't in the budget, then use stock image websites like

- Shutterstock: www.shutterstock.com
- iStock: www.istockphoto.com
- Adobe Stock: www.stock.adobe.com
- Getty Images: www.gettyimages.com
- Unsplash: www.unsplash.com
- Pexels: www.pexels.com

Be picky about the images you choose to represent your business or organization's brand. Ensure the colors and the style of the images work together and are cohesive and compelling.

Infographics effectively present complex information in a visually engaging manner. They simplify data, making it more accessible and understandable to your audience. Videos, on the other hand, can be highly informative and entertaining. They can capture visitors' attention and encourage them to spend more

While visuals are important, pretty, and flashy, you can't overestimate the importance of load speed.

time on your website. If utilized strategically, videos can enhance your brand storytelling efforts and forge a deeper connection with your target audience.

While visuals are important, pretty, and flashy, you can't overestimate the importance of load speed. If your website takes too long to load, visitors will leave, no matter how beautiful it is. Finding the right balance between captivating visuals and fast load times is crucial to creating a user-friendly home page with a seamless browsing experience.

About Page

Your Origin Story: When it comes to your About Us page, storytelling becomes a potent tool for forging connections and nurturing trust with your audience. By sharing your business's origin story, you're inviting readers to join you on your journey. They'll learn about the inspiration behind your facility, the challenges you've faced, and the triumphs you've celebrated. This personal touch humanizes your brand and makes it relatable to your audience. They'll feel like they're getting to know you on a deeper level, which can foster a sense of trust and loyalty.

Don't shy away from sharing the obstacles you've encountered. Everyone appreciates an underdog story, and by being open about your struggles, you can make your brand more relatable and inspiring. It demonstrates that you're not infallible but resolute in your quest for success. This, in turn, showcases your resilience and tenacity, qualities that customers admire in a business.

When you tell your story, be authentic and passionate. Let your personality shine through, and don't be afraid to show some emotion. The more genuine you are, the more your audience will connect with you. Your story makes you stand out from the competition, so take the time to craft it carefully and share it with pride.

Showcase Your Team: Your About Us page is a great place to showcase the talented people who make your company unique—

your team. You can create a personal connection that resonates with your audience by introducing your team members and providing insights into their roles, backgrounds, and interests.

When writing team bios, include the team member's role, relevant background information, and a bit of personality through interests or anecdotes. This approach will help potential clients understand your team's breadth of skills and expertise and give them a sense of your company's culture. Anecdotes or stories can be especially compelling for illustrating your team's values and helping readers feel connected.

Only some people like having their pictures taken, but quality photos are vital to a website that maximizes the user experience. So, even though it might be as painful as pulling teeth, professional headshots are a must. This bears repeating, especially for your key team members: getting professional headshots is worth the investment! Thoughtful and consistent team photos help to humanize your brand and make it easier for potential customers to remember and connect with you.

Thoughtful and consistent team photos help to humanize your brand and make it easier for potential customers to remember and connect with you.

If you want to take things to the next level, have each provider record a short video (no more than 30-45 seconds) to put with their bio. It can even be a brief, heartfelt welcome message. These videos go even deeper in their connections with potential clients and help people who are anxious about seeking help feel more comfortable.

Include Client Testimonials: By showcasing the positive experiences of your satisfied former clients, you are essentially letting your clients do the talking for you, building trust and credibility genuinely and authentically. When it comes to showcasing testimonials, authenticity is critical, so encourage former clients to share their thoughts in their own words. As mentioned before, this can be more tricky with mental or behavioral health clinics, but this makes them even more powerful when done respectfully and in compliance with HIPAA regulations. You cannot approach current clients about reviews or client testimonials, but you can ask former clients if they are interested in talking about their experiences.

It is also critical to include direct quotes, logos, or the names of well-known companies or people who have supported your business. These endorsements act as social proof, reinforcing the credibility of your brand and increasing the likelihood of conversion.

Services or Products Pages

Service or product pages are crucial because they provide detailed information about your facility's offers, directly influencing visitors' decisions. These pages are essential for educating potential clients about how your products or services can help them with their challenges. They also play a key role in improving search engine optimization (SEO) by incorporating relevant keywords that attract targeted traffic. Well-crafted product or service pages can enhance user experience, build trust, and ultimately drive conversions to new appointments for your clinicians.

If you're considering using paid ads on platforms like Google, Facebook, Instagram, YouTube, TikTok, LinkedIn, etc., creating dedicated pages for each product or service you advertise is crucial. When users click on an ad, they expect to land on a page that provides detailed information about what was advertised, not a generic home or about us page. This targeted approach helps meet user expectations and enhances the effectiveness of your ads.

FAQs or Resources Section: This section addresses common client questions and provides additional resources, helping to reduce customer service inquiries and enhance user satisfaction.

Contact Information: Easy access to contact details is crucial. This should include a dedicated Contact page with multiple ways to reach your business, such as a contact form, phone number, and physical address.

Social Media Links: Integrating direct links to your social media profiles encourages users to engage with your brand across different platforms, enhancing your online community and presence.

Call to Action (CTA) Buttons: Strategically placed CTAs guide users to valuable actions for your practice, such as signing up for newsletters, booking an appointment, or contacting you for more details.

Privacy Policy and Terms of Service: These are critical for compliance and transparency. They inform users about your data handling practices and your website's terms of service.

These elements are designed to enhance user experience by providing precise and intuitive pathways for navigation. They ensure users can easily find their needs and take desired actions without confusion.

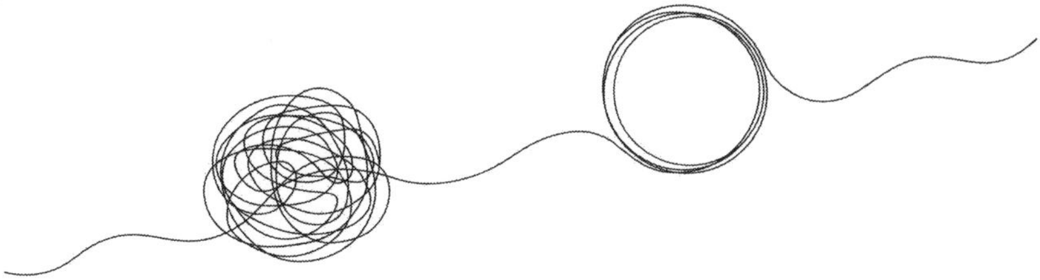

Chapter 5: Content Marketing

Blogging is vital for mental and behavioral health marketing as it provides a platform to establish thought leadership, share valuable insights, and connect with your target audience. Through informative and engaging blog posts, clinics can educate potential clients about mental health issues, treatment options, and the importance of seeking help. Blogging also helps improve search engine visibility, driving organic traffic to the website and enhancing the clinic's online presence. By consistently publishing high-quality content, mental and behavioral health clinics can build credibility, foster trust with their audience, and ultimately attract more clients.

The most important elements for quality blogging include several vital aspects that ensure your blog or article is engaging, informative, and optimized for search engines. Here's a detailed breakdown of these elements:

Engaging Content: Your blog posts should be valuable and interesting. This involves creating content relevant to your audience's interests and needs that aligns with your brand's messaging and goals. Engaging content often includes informative text, compelling narratives, and practical advice.

SEO Optimization: Properly optimizing your blog posts for search engines is crucial. This includes using relevant keywords naturally throughout the content, optimizing meta tags and descriptions, and structuring the content with appropriate headers. SEO helps in improving your blog's visibility and search engine rankings.

Scannable Format: Your blog posts should be formatted to be easy to read. Use short paragraphs, bullet points, and subheadings to break up text and make the content more digestible. This not only enhances readability but also helps keep the reader's attention.

Consistency: Posting blogs regularly is critical to maintaining and growing your audience. Your blogging schedule should be consistent, telling your readers when to expect new content, which can help build a loyal readership over time. You don't necessarily have to post a blog every week; it can be once or twice a month if that works for you. The most important thing is to pick a cadence you can keep up with and stick to it.

Call-to-Actions (CTAs): Each blog post should have a clear call to action. Whether it's encouraging readers to comment, share the post, read related articles, or book an appointment, CTAs guide users to the next steps and help convert readers into leads or clients.

Use of Visuals: Incorporating images, videos, or infographics within your blog posts can significantly enhance their appeal and effectiveness. Visuals help to illustrate points, break up text, and make the content more engaging and memorable.

Quality and Depth: Your blog posts should be well-researched and thorough. High-quality, in-depth content that provides valuable insights and information tends to perform better in terms of both reader engagement and SEO.

Where to Find Good Blogging Ideas

Keyword Research: Utilizing tools like SEMRush, Ahrefs, SpyFu, Ubersuggest, Google Search Console, and Moz Pro can help you identify what topics are trending in your industry, what your audience is searching for, and how you can tailor your content to meet those needs. This research will guide you in creating relevant content likely to attract organic traffic.

Customer Questions and Feedback: Listening to your audience's questions and feedback can provide direct insights into their interests. This can be a rich source of ideas for blog posts that address their specific concerns and needs.

Competitor Analysis: Observing the types of content your competitors publish can give you ideas on what topics resonate with the audience in your industry. This doesn't mean copying their content, but rather understanding the gaps in their content that you could fill or identifying aspects that you can execute differently or better.

Current Events and Industry News: Staying updated with industry news and current events can provide timely topics for blog posts. This keeps your content relevant and positions your blog as a go-to resource for fresh and topical information.

Internal Expertise: Leverage your organization's knowledge and expertise. Interviews with your various practitioners or guest posts from different departments can provide unique perspectives and deep insights into specific topics related to your field.

Analytical Tools: Utilizing Google Analytics can help you understand which types of content perform best on your blog. This data can inform your future content creation, allowing you to focus on the topics and formats that engage your audience the most.

By combining these strategies, you can develop a robust source of ideas for your blogging content, enhance your SEO efforts, and significantly boost engagement with your target audience.

Can AI Help Write Articles?

Using AI to write blogs can be valuable in your content creation strategy, especially when combined with human oversight and creativity. Remember you are marketing to and connecting with humans, not AI. Using AI to generate research and the framework is a good start, but you must humanize it.

Here are a few considerations to keep in mind if you decide to incorporate AI into your blogging strategy:

Human Touch: While AI can generate content based on data and predefined parameters, it lacks the human touch to make it genuinely engaging and relatable. Reviewing and editing AI-generated content to ensure it aligns with your brand's voice and meets your audience's expectations is non-negotiable. Use personalized stories and perspectives to add that human touch. It is not acceptable to copy and paste AI-generated content into your blog.

As of the writing of this book in 2024, AI-generated content cannot be copyrighted by an individual or company, so unless you modify it with your insights and perspectives, you do not own the content. At present, it is not just a relatability issue but also a legal one that requires us to humanize any AI-generated content.

SEO Optimization: AI tools can help optimize content for SEO by suggesting relevant keywords, generating meta descriptions, and even analyzing the effectiveness of your headlines. However, a person who understands SEO deeply should manage the strategic placement of these elements and ensure they fit naturally within your content.

Originality and Creativity: AI can sometimes produce generic content that might not stand out in a crowded digital landscape. Human creativity is essential to develop unique angles, compelling narratives, and innovative ideas that capture attention and engage readers.

Accuracy and Fact-Checking: AI may not always provide accurate or up-to-date information, especially if the input data is flawed or limited. Human oversight is crucial to verify facts, update outdated information, and ensure the overall accuracy of your blog posts.

Incorporating AI into your blogging strategy can increase efficiency and help with certain aspects of content creation. Still, it works best when complemented by human expertise and creativity to ensure quality and effectiveness.

Title Tags and Meta Descriptions

Are title tags and meta descriptions really that important for blogging? Yes, they are! Meta descriptions and title tags are essential components of a successful blog strategy. By optimizing these elements with relevant keywords, compelling language, and accurate descriptions, you can improve your blog's visibility, attract more organic traffic, and enhance user engagement.

Improved Click-Through Rates: A well-crafted meta description and title tag can entice users to click on your blog when it appears on search engine results pages (SERPs). They provide a brief summary of your content, giving users a preview of what to expect. A compelling meta description and title tag can increase click-through rates and drive more traffic to your blog.

SEO Benefits: Title tags and meta descriptions are important ranking factors for search engines. Search engines use these elements to understand your blog's content and determine its relevance to user search queries. Including relevant keywords in your title tag and meta description can help improve your blog's visibility in search results.

Brand Visibility and Credibility: Consistent and well-crafted title tags and meta descriptions can help build brand visibility and credibility. When users consistently see your blog appearing in search results with informative and engaging meta descriptions, it can establish trust and recognition for your brand.

Title tags and meta descriptions help users quickly understand your blog's content and whether it meets their needs. Clear and relevant descriptions can attract the right audience to your blog and help reduce bounce rates.

Social Sharing: When your blog posts are shared on social media platforms, the title tag and meta description are often used as the preview text. Having compelling and informative meta descriptions can encourage social media users to click on your shared posts and visit your blog.

Quality Sources of Photographs and Illustrations

Bloggers and website owners can use several quality illustration and photography sources to enhance their content. Some popular sources include:

- **Adobe Stock:** Adobe Stock is a reputable platform that offers a vast collection of high-quality stock photos, illustrations, vectors, and videos for commercial and personal use. Users can purchase and download images directly from the Adobe Stock website.
- **Shutterstock:** Shutterstock is one of the largest stock photography websites, offering millions of images, illustrations, videos, and music tracks for licensing. Users

can search for and purchase images based on their specific needs and preferences.

- **Unsplash**: Unsplash is a popular platform for free high-resolution photos contributed by photographers around the world. Users can browse and download images for free, making it an excellent resource for bloggers and website owners looking for high-quality, visually appealing photos.
- **Pexels**: Pexels is another free stock photo platform that offers a wide range of high-quality images and videos for personal and commercial use. Users can search for photos based on categories or keywords and download them for free.
- **Freepik**: Freepik is a popular resource for free and premium vector graphics, illustrations, and photos. Users can find a variety of designs and images to enhance their blog posts and website content.
- **Canva**: Canva is a graphic design platform that offers a wide range of design elements, including illustrations, photos, templates, and graphics. Users can create custom designs or use pre-made templates to enhance their blog and website content.
- **StockSnap.io**: StockSnap.io is a free stock photo website that offers high-quality images for personal and commercial use. Users can search for photos based on categories, keywords, and popularity and download them for free.

These are just a few illustration and photography sources for bloggers and website owners to use in their content. Whether you need free or premium images, there are plenty of options to enhance the visual appeal of your blog posts and website content.

Quality website content is…

Quality content is a critical marketing component for a mental or behavioral health website as it is a powerful tool to educate, engage, and connect with your target audience. Well-crafted content that is informative, empathetic, and relevant can help build trust with visitors, establish your clinic's expertise, and showcase its commitment to providing valuable resources and support. Quality content not only improves the website's visibility and search engine ranking but also enhances the user experience and ultimately drives conversions.

Well-crafted web content is informative, empathetic, and relevant

---

By consistently delivering high-quality content that addresses the needs and concerns of individuals seeking mental health information and services, your website can effectively differentiate itself in a competitive market and attract and retain clients and high-quality talent. The most critical elements of quality content for your website focus on several key aspects that enhance user engagement and SEO effectiveness. Here's a detailed look at these elements:

Relevance and Authority: Your content should be highly relevant to your target audience's needs and interests. It should position your brand as an authority in your field, providing valuable information that addresses your audience's questions and concerns. This helps build trust and credibility.

Engagement: The content should be engaging and written to capture and retain the reader's attention. This can be achieved through a compelling narrative, interesting facts, or interactive elements that encourage active participation from the audience.

SEO Optimization: It is crucial to incorporate SEO strategies into your content. This includes using appropriate keywords naturally, optimizing meta tags and descriptions, and structuring content with proper headers to improve readability and search engine rankings.

Visual Appeal: Incorporating visual elements like images, videos, and infographics can significantly enhance the appeal of your content. These elements help break up text, illustrate points, and provide a more engaging and digestible format for complex information.

Clear Call to Action: Your content should always have a clear call to action (CTA). Whether it's encouraging readers to contact you, subscribe to a newsletter, or follow you on social media, CTAs guide users toward the next steps, helping to convert interest into action.

Comprehensive and Detailed: Content that delves deeply into topics (usually 1,200-2,000 words per blog or article) tends to perform better in terms of SEO and user engagement. Detailed content that covers topics extensively can improve your site's authority and keep readers engaged longer.

Updated and Accurate: It is vital to ensure that your content is up-to-date and accurate. This helps maintain your site's credibility and keeps your content relevant in the rapidly changing digital landscape.

Email Marketing

Email marketing is an effective tool for mental or behavioral health clinics as it allows them to engage with their audience in a personalized and targeted manner. By sending informative and relevant content directly to subscribers' inboxes, clinics can nurture relationships, provide valuable resources, and promote their services non-intrusively. Email campaigns can educate clients about mental health topics, share success stories, announce events or new services, and encourage appointments or consultations. With the ability to segment email lists, track engagement metrics, and automate campaigns, email marketing enables clinics to reach the right audience at the right time, foster trust and loyalty, and ultimately drive conversions and retention.

The six critical elements of a quality marketing email are:

Personalization: Personalization goes beyond addressing the recipient by their name. It involves tailoring the email content to align with the recipient's preferences, behaviors, and past interactions with your brand. This could include personalized service recommendations, content, or focused articles based on their engagement with previous emails or which provider they see.

Clear and Compelling Subject Lines: The subject line is the gateway to your email content. A compelling subject line should be concise, clear, and intriguing enough to prompt the recipient to open the email. It should hint at what to expect in the email while creating a sense of urgency or curiosity. Testing different subject lines can help identify what effectively captures your audience's attention.

Valuable Content: Your email content should offer real value to the recipient. This could be informative content, exclusive deals, insightful news about your products or services, or helpful tips related to the recipient's interests. The key is to ensure that the content is relevant and provides a reason for the recipient to engage further with your brand.

Strong Call-to-Action (CTA): A clear and compelling call to action is crucial for driving the recipient toward the desired action. The CTA should be visually distinct and placed strategically within the email to catch the reader's attention. It should use action-oriented language that leaves no doubt about what the recipient should do next, whether it's making a purchase, signing up for a webinar, or following a link to read more.

Responsive Design: With a significant number of emails being opened on mobile devices, your email design must be responsive. This means ensuring the email content displays correctly across different devices and screen sizes. A responsive design improves the user experience and increases the likelihood of engagement with the email content.

Testing and Optimization: Continuous testing and optimization are vital for improving the effectiveness of your email campaigns. This involves A/B testing various elements of your email, such as the subject line, design, content, and CTAs, to see what resonates best with your audience. Analyzing the results of these tests can provide valuable insights that help refine your email strategy, ensuring better performance in future campaigns.

By focusing on these elements, you can create marketing emails that reach and resonate with your audience, encouraging them to take action and engage with your brand.

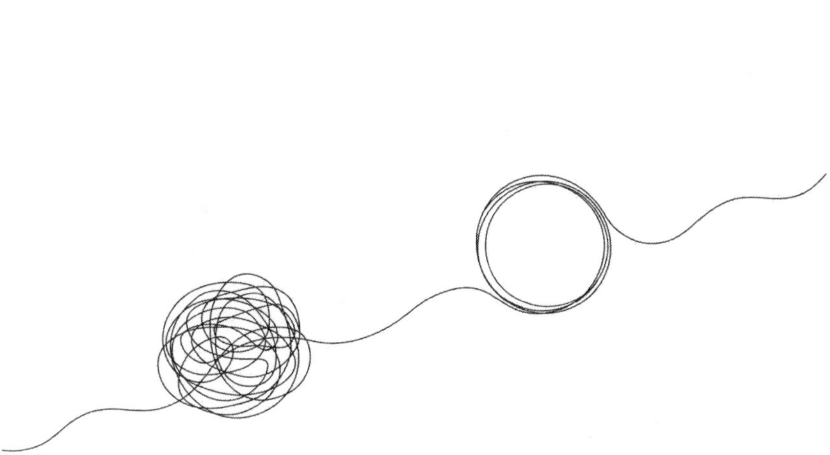

Chapter 6: Organic Social Media Marketing

Social media posting is a crucial component of a robust marketing plan for mental or behavioral health practices. It provides a platform to connect with the community, raise awareness, and engage with current and potential clients. By sharing informative and engaging content on social media platforms, clinics can reach a wider audience, drive traffic to their website, and foster meaningful conversations around mental health topics.

Social media posting allows you to showcase your expertise, share testimonials, promote events or services, and humanize your brand, building trust and credibility with followers. With the ability to interact in real-time, respond to inquiries, and share resources, social media posting is vital in building relationships, increasing visibility, and establishing the clinic as a trusted resource for mental health support and information.

One of the things to keep in mind is that not all channels are going to be ideal for your practice. Remember the target audience work we did at the beginning of this book? This is another place where it comes into play. Picking which social media channels you want to post content comes down to understanding which of them your target audience prefers, as well as the pros and cons of each. Once you have both in mind, you can make educated decisions on which to use. Check out some of the resources at the back of this book for data on social media channel users from the Pew Institute.

That being said, there are important principles to remember for social media marketing that are not channel-specific, including:

Understanding Your Audience: Knowing who you are targeting is crucial. This involves creating detailed buyer personas that reflect your audience's demographics, interests, and behaviors. This ensures your content is tailored and relevant, increasing engagement and effectiveness.

Your social media profiles and posts should consistently reflect your brand's visual and verbal identity.

Consistency in Branding: Your social media profiles and posts should consistently reflect your brand's visual and verbal identity. This includes using consistent logos, color schemes, and messaging that aligns with your brand's values and overall marketing strategy. Consistency helps in building brand recognition and trust among your audience.

Engagement: Social media is not just a broadcasting platform; it's a two-way communication channel. Engage with your audience by responding to comments, participating in conversations, and encouraging user-generated content. This helps build a community and foster loyalty.

Utilizing the Right Platforms: Not all social media platforms suit your brand. Choose platforms that best align with your buyer personas' preferences and where they are most active. This targeted approach helps you utilize your resources more effectively.

Leveraging Multimedia: Using videos, images, and other multimedia content can significantly enhance engagement on social media. These formats are often more effective in catching attention and conveying your message than text-only posts.

Analytics and Adaptation: Use analytics tools to track the performance of your social media activities. Analyze what types of content perform best, at what times, and with which segments of your audience. Use this data to refine your strategies and improve effectiveness.

Regular Updates and Fresh Content: Keep your content fresh and updated. Regular posting keeps your audience engaged and helps maintain visibility in the crowded social media landscape.

Now that you have a 20,000-foot view of social media principles, let's examine the pros and cons of the primary channels.

Facebook (Meta)

Marketing on Facebook offers numerous benefits for mental or behavioral health clinics, providing a powerful platform to reach and engage with a targeted audience. With over two billion active users, Facebook allows clinics like yours to showcase their services, share educational content, and connect with individuals seeking mental health support. You can reach specific demographics, interests, or behaviors through targeted advertising, ensuring your message reaches the right audience.

Facebook's analytics tools also provide valuable insights into marketing campaigns' performance, allowing you to optimize your strategies and maximize the return on investment. By leveraging Facebook's reach, targeting capabilities, and analytics tools, your practice can effectively raise awareness, attract new clients, and build a community of support online.

Pros and Cons

Organic content marketing on Facebook involves creating and sharing valuable, engaging content with your audience without paying for advertising. While organic content marketing can effectively reach and engage with your target audience, it has pros and cons. Here are some of the key pros and cons of organic content marketing on Facebook:

Pros of Facebook:

Cost-effective: Organic content marketing on Facebook is a cost-effective way to reach your audience without paying for advertising. It requires an investment of time over cash, making it a budget-friendly option for businesses looking to build brand awareness and engage with clients and potential clients.

Builds brand credibility: By consistently sharing valuable and relevant content with your audience, you can build trust and credibility for your brand. Providing helpful information and engaging with your followers can help establish your brand as an authority in the mental and behavioral health industries.

Increases organic reach: Well-crafted and engaging content has the potential to reach a wider audience organically through likes, shares, and comments. When your audience engages with your content, it can help increase visibility and reach on Facebook.

Fosters community engagement: Organic content marketing allows you to interact with your audience in a more personalized way. You can build a sense of community and loyalty among your followers by responding to comments, addressing questions, and fostering discussions.

Cons of Facebook:

Declining organic reach: Over the years, Facebook's algorithm has prioritized content from family and friends over business pages, leading to a decline in organic reach for business posts. This means your organic content may not reach as many people as it used to. You can overcome this with boosted posts.

Time-consuming: Creating and managing organic content on Facebook can be time-consuming. It requires planning, creating, and optimizing content regularly to engage your audience. This can be challenging for a clinic with limited resources or without someone passionate about mental health and social media.

Limited targeting options: Organic content marketing on Facebook does not offer the same targeting options as paid advertising. This means that you may not be able to reach specific segments of your target audience as effectively through organic content alone.

Uncertain results: Unlike paid advertising, the results of organic content marketing on Facebook can be less predictable. Seeing tangible results regarding increased engagement, website traffic, or conversions may take time.

While organic Facebook posting can be a cost-effective way to build brand credibility and engage with your audience, it may also face challenges such as declining organic reach and limited targeting options. We recommend combining organic and paid strategies to maximize reach and engagement on Facebook.

Instagram

Instagram is an effective marketing tool for your mental health or behavioral health practice due to its visual nature and engaged user base. By sharing visually appealing content such as inspirational quotes, mental health tips, self-care practices, and success stories, clinics can connect with their audience on a personal and emotional level. Instagram's features, such as Stories, IGTV, and Reels, provide opportunities to share authentic, behind-the-scenes glimpses of your clinic (think waiting area, play therapy rooms, etc), showcase staff expertise, and engage with followers creatively and interactively. With hashtags, geotags, and targeted advertising, clinics can expand their reach, attract new clients, and raise awareness about mental health issues. Instagram's emphasis on community and connection makes it a valuable platform for mental health practices to build trust, foster engagement, and promote mental well-being in a visually compelling manner.

Pros of Instagram:

Organic posting on Instagram as a marketing tool for mental or behavioral health practices offers several advantages:

Authentic Connection: Organic posts allow clinics to share genuine, authentic content that resonates with their audience, fostering a deeper connection and building trust with followers.

Cost-Effective: Organic posting is a cost-effective way to reach and engage with followers without the need for paid advertising, making it accessible for practices with limited marketing budgets.

Boosted Posts Available: Instagram allows boosted posts through its advertising platform, which is integrated with Facebook Ads Manager. By boosting a post on Instagram, you can increase the reach and visibility of your content to a targeted audience beyond your existing followers. Boosted posts appear in users' feeds as sponsored content and can be customized with specific objectives, targeting criteria, budget, and duration. This feature enables you to promote important announcements, educational content, services, events, or other relevant information to a broader audience, driving engagement, website traffic, and potential client inquiries.

Relationship Building: Clinics can build relationships with their audience, encourage engagement, and cultivate community around their brand by consistently posting valuable content.

Brand Awareness: Organic posts help increase brand visibility and awareness among followers and attract new followers interested in mental health topics and services. This is an excellent platform to showcase your values, mission, and unique approach to client care. You can communicate your commitment to supporting mental well-being through visually engaging content and compelling storytelling.

Content Strategy: Organic posting allows clinics to develop a content strategy tailored to their target audience's needs and interests, providing valuable information, resources, and support for mental health and well-being.

Organic posting on Instagram for mental or behavioral health practices can also help establish thought leadership. By consistently sharing insightful content, tips, and resources related to mental health, clinics can position themselves as experts and trusted sources of information within the industry. This can further enhance their credibility and authority, attracting followers who value the expertise and guidance provided by the clinic.

Organic posting on Instagram for mental or behavioral health practices can also help establish thought leadership.

Cons of Instagram:

While organic posting on Instagram can be a valuable marketing tool for mental or behavioral health practices, there are some potential drawbacks to consider:

Limited Reach: Organic posts may have limited reach compared to paid advertising or boosted posts, as they rely on the platform's algorithm to show content to followers. This can make it challenging to reach a wider audience and attract new followers to your clinic's profile.

Time and Resources: Consistently creating and posting high-quality content on Instagram requires time, effort, and resources. For smaller practices or clinics with limited staff, maintaining a regular posting schedule and engaging with followers may be time-consuming and detract from your other essential tasks.

Algorithm Changes: Instagram's algorithm frequently changes, affecting how posts are prioritized and displayed in users' feeds. This can impact the visibility and engagement of organic posts, making it challenging for you to predict how their content will perform and reach their target audience.

Competition and Saturation: The platform is highly competitive, with millions of businesses and individuals vying for attention. The saturation of content on Instagram can make it challenging for your practice to stand out and capture the interest of their followers amidst the sea of posts.

Limited Analytics: Organic posts on Instagram may not provide as detailed analytics and insights as paid advertising or promoted posts. This can make it harder for clinics to track the performance of their content, understand their audience's preferences, and optimize their marketing strategies effectively.

Limited link options: Instagram offers limited options for linking back to websites. Only one clickable link is allowed in the bio, and swipe-up links in Stories are available only to accounts with 10,000 followers or more.

YouTube

YouTube can be a highly effective platform for mental or behavioral health marketing, providing practices with a powerful medium to educate, engage, and connect with a broad audience. Through video content, practices can share valuable information, tips, resources, and personal stories that resonate with viewers seeking mental health support and guidance.

YouTube's visual format allows practices to convey complex mental health concepts in an engaging and accessible way, making it easier for viewers to understand and connect with the content. By creating a library of educational videos, expert interviews, therapy techniques, and self-care tips, practices can establish themselves as trusted authorities in the field and build credibility with viewers. Furthermore, YouTube's reach and discoverability enable practices to expand their online presence, attract new clients, and raise awareness about mental health issues and services, ultimately making a positive impact in the mental health space through engaging and informative video content.

That being said, the challenge we most often see for clinics is having the time to plan, coordinate, shoot, edit, and publish enough video content to be effective on this platform. For facilities with the interest and resources to take on this social channel, it can be a powerful part of their overall marketing campaign.

Pros of YouTube:

Visual Content: Video content is engaging and can convey complex mental health concepts, stories, and messages in a compelling and accessible way. Mental health practices can share educational information, personal stories, therapy techniques, and self-care tips through videos to connect with viewers on a deeper level.

Reach and Visibility: YouTube is one of the largest video-sharing platforms globally, with millions of users consuming video content daily. By creating and optimizing videos for search and discovery, mental health practices can reach a wider audience, attract new clients, and raise awareness about mental health issues and services.

Educational Resources: YouTube allows behavioral health practices to create a library of educational resources, tutorials, webinars, and expert interviews that provide valuable information and support to viewers seeking mental health guidance. These resources can help establish the practice as a trusted authority in the field.

Engagement and Interaction: Through comments, discussions, and community engagement, YouTube enables two-way communication between mental health practices and viewers. Practices can respond to viewer questions, provide support, and foster community and connection through video content.

Brand Building: Behavioral health practices can build brand awareness, credibility, and trust among viewers by consistently creating high-quality and informative videos. Video content humanizes the practice, showcases its expertise, and establishes a strong online presence that resonates with individuals seeking mental health resources and support.

Overall, YouTube offers mental health practices a powerful platform to share valuable content, reach a diverse audience, and positively impact mental health through engaging and informative video content.

Cons of YouTube:

Privacy Concerns: Behavioral and mental health clinics must be mindful of patient privacy and confidentiality when creating video content on YouTube. It is vital to remember HIPAA regulations when sharing personal stories or sensitive information in videos. Ensuring compliance with these regulations while creating and sharing video content on YouTube can be challenging.

Reaching the Target Audience: With millions of videos uploaded to YouTube daily, you might find it challenging to stand out and reach the target audience. Creating engaging and optimized content that resonates with viewers interested in mental health topics requires time, effort, and a strategic approach.

Negative Comments and Feedback: YouTube's open comment section allows for viewer interaction, but it also allows for negative comments, feedback, or trolling. If you post on YouTube, you must monitor and manage comments carefully to maintain a positive and supportive online environment.

Brand Reputation Risks: In the digital age, online reputation management is crucial for businesses, including behavioral and mental health clinics. Negative content, misinformation, or controversies associated with YouTube videos can impact the clinic's brand reputation and credibility.

Limited Control Over Ad Placement: When you post your videos on YouTube, you don't necessarily have control over what ads run before or during your videos. This lack of control can result in ads being displayed alongside unrelated or potentially inappropriate content.

YouTube offers many benefits and drawbacks to marketing for your mental or behavioral health clinic. Please consider them both before committing to posting on the channel. Remember, consistency is key, so weigh the costs before you start.

Pinterest

Pinterest offers numerous benefits for reaching and engaging with a diverse audience seeking mental wellness resources and support. Similar to Instagram, Pinterest is an ideal visual discovery platform for clinics to share visually appealing content such as inspirational quotes, self-care tips, therapy techniques, and mental health resources in a visually engaging format.

By targeting users interested in mental health, mindfulness, and self-improvement, you can reach a relevant and receptive audience seeking mental health information and services. Pinterest also serves as a traffic and referral source, driving users to clinic websites and blogs through shared pins and links, increasing brand visibility, and attracting potential clients. By consistently sharing valuable and informative content on Pinterest, mental and behavioral health clinics can build brand awareness, credibility, and trust among users, positioning themselves as trusted authorities in the mental health industry.

This act of sharing not only builds your facility's brand but also empowers you to make a significant impact in the mental health community.

Additionally, fostering community engagement through shared boards and interactions allows clinics to create a supportive and interactive space where users can connect, share experiences, and access valuable mental health resources, ultimately making a positive impact in the mental health community.

Pros of Pinterest

Visual Content Sharing: Pinterest is a visual discovery platform, making it ideal for showcasing visually impactful content such as infographics, inspirational quotes, therapeutic techniques, self-care tips, and mental health resources. Visual content can be highly engaging and resonate with users seeking mental health information and support.

Targeted Audience Reach: Pinterest allows for precise audience targeting based on interests, demographics, and behaviors, enabling you to reach users interested in mental wellness, self-improvement, mindfulness, and related topics. This targeted approach can help attract individuals seeking mental health resources and services, which makes it even more important to know and understand your target audience on a deep level.

Traffic and Referral Opportunities: Pinterest can drive traffic to your website or blogs through shared pins and links, increasing brand visibility and attracting potential clients. By creating engaging and informative content on Pinterest, companies can generate leads and referrals to your website.

Brand Awareness and Credibility: Mental health companies can build brand awareness, credibility, and trust among users by consistently sharing valuable and relevant content on Pinterest. Establishing a presence on Pinterest as a go-to resource for mental health information can position you as an authority in the industry.

Community Engagement: Pinterest allows for community engagement through shared boards, comments, and interactions with users interested in mental health topics. Companies can foster a supportive and interactive community on Pinterest, encouraging dialogue, sharing experiences, and providing emotional support to users seeking mental health resources. This sense of community can make users feel connected and supported, enhancing their overall experience on the platform.

Cons of Pinterest

Privacy Concerns: Mental and behavioral health practices must prioritize patient privacy and confidentiality when sharing content on Pinterest. Posting sensitive information, personal stories, or therapy techniques can inadvertently compromise patient confidentiality and violate ethical guidelines. Therefore, it is critical to observe all HIPAA regulations when producing content to share on Pinterest.

Misinterpretation of Content: Visual content shared on Pinterest may be open to interpretation, potentially leading to misunderstandings or misinterpretations of mental health information, resources, or practices. Clinics must ensure that the content they share is accurate, clear, and contextually appropriate to avoid confusion or misinformation.

Limited Reach: While Pinterest can be effective for reaching users interested in mental health and wellness, the platform may have a more niche audience compared to other social media platforms. You may find it challenging to reach a broader demographic or specific target audience beyond Pinterest's user base.

Managing Engagement: Pinterest's interactive features, such as comments and community engagement, require active management to monitor feedback, respond to inquiries, and foster a supportive online environment. As with most social media platforms, you must have someone qualified and committed to engage with users effectively and address any questions or concerns that may arise.

Brand Reputation Risks: Negative comments, feedback, or controversies associated with Pinterest content can potentially impact a mental health practice's brand reputation and credibility. Maintaining a positive and professional online presence on Pinterest is essential to mitigate reputation risks.

While Pinterest can be a valuable platform for marketing mental and behavioral health practices, clinics must carefully navigate these potential cons, uphold patient privacy and confidentiality, ensure regulatory compliance, and manage their online presence effectively to leverage the platform's benefits while mitigating risks.

Overall, marketing on Pinterest can be an effective strategy for mental and behavioral health companies to connect with their target audience, raise awareness about mental health topics, and establish a trusted and engaging online presence within the mental health community. By leveraging the platform's features, clinics can ensure that their audience is well-informed and enlightened about mental health issues.

Twitter (X)

Organic posting on Twitter for mental health marketing offers several benefits for your clinic if you want to engage with your audience, raise awareness, and build a support community. Through organic tweets, clinics can share valuable content, resources, tips, and insights related to mental health topics, positioning themselves as trusted sources of information and support within the industry. By fostering conversations, responding to inquiries, and actively engaging with followers, clinics can create a dynamic and interactive online presence that encourages dialogue, connection, and empathy.

Organic posting on Twitter allows clinics to showcase their personality, values, and expertise, humanizing their brand and establishing a relatable and authentic voice that resonates with their audience. Additionally, by leveraging hashtags, retweets, and trending topics, clinics can increase the visibility of their tweets, reach a wider audience, and amplify their impact on the mental health community.

Pros of Twitter:

Real-Time Engagement: Twitter is a real-time platform allowing practices to instantly engage with their audience. By participating in conversations, responding to inquiries, and sharing timely updates, clinics can establish a solid online presence and connect with followers meaningfully.

Thought Leadership: Twitter is a platform where clinics can share expertise, insights, and resources related to mental health topics. By sharing valuable content, clinics can position themselves as thought leaders in the field, attract followers seeking information and support, and build credibility within the industry.

Community Building: Twitter enables practices to build a community of followers interested in mental health, well-being, and self-care. By sharing relatable content, fostering discussions, and amplifying voices within the community, clinics can create a supportive online environment that resonates with their target audience.

Networking and Collaboration: Twitter provides opportunities for clinics to network with other mental health professionals, organizations, and advocates. By engaging with like-minded individuals and participating in relevant conversations, clinics can expand their reach, forge partnerships, and collaborate on initiatives that promote mental health awareness and advocacy.

Cons of Twitter:

Character Limit: Twitter's character limit of 280 characters per tweet can be restrictive for users who want to share longer or more detailed content. Users may find it challenging to convey complex ideas or messages within the character limit.

Information Overload: Twitter's fast-paced and constantly updating feed can lead to information overload for users. Keeping up with a high volume of tweets, news, and conversations can be overwhelming and time-consuming.

Trolls and Harassment: Like other social media platforms, Twitter is not immune to online harassment, bullying, and abusive behavior. Users may encounter trolls and toxic comments, which can negatively impact their experience on the platform.

Fake News and Misinformation: Twitter has been criticized for its role in spreading fake news, misinformation, and disinformation. Users must be vigilant about verifying sources and fact-checking information shared on the platform.

Algorithm Changes: Twitter's algorithm updates and changes can affect the visibility and reach of users' tweets. Changes in the algorithm can impact engagement, followers, and overall performance on the platform.

Twitter offers numerous benefits, such as real-time updates, broad reach, engagement opportunities, brand building, and networking. However, the platform's limitations and challenges include character limit, information overload, trolls and harassment, fake news, misinformation, and algorithm changes.

LinkedIn

LinkedIn can be highly effective for mental and behavioral health facilities seeking to reach a professional audience, establish credibility, and connect with relevant stakeholders in the healthcare industry. LinkedIn's focus on professional networking and B2B interactions makes it an ideal platform for showcasing the expertise, services and thought leadership of mental health facilities to a targeted audience of healthcare professionals, therapists, counselors, and potential partners. By sharing informative articles, research findings, success stories, and industry insights, mental health facilities can position themselves as leaders in the field and build trust among professionals seeking mental health resources and collaborations.

LinkedIn's focus on professional networking and B2B interactions makes it an ideal platform for showcasing the expertise, services, and thought leadership of your mental health facility

LinkedIn also offers opportunities for networking, engaging in discussions, and forming partnerships within the healthcare community. This enables facilities to expand their professional network, attract referrals, appeal to potential employees, and raise awareness about their services in a professional and reputable environment. Marketing on LinkedIn can help your mental or behavioral health clinic enhance your brand visibility, establish industry authority, and foster valuable connections within the healthcare sector.

Pros of LinkedIn:

Professional Audience Targeting: LinkedIn provides mental and behavioral health clinics with access to a professional audience, including therapists, counselors, psychologists, and healthcare professionals. This allows you to target your marketing efforts towards individuals who may be interested in job opportunities, professional collaborations, or career advancement within the mental health field.

Recruitment Marketing Opportunities: LinkedIn's robust recruitment marketing features, such as job postings, career pages, and targeted job ads, make it an effective platform for attracting top talent to mental health clinics. You can showcase your workplace culture, job openings, employee testimonials, and career development opportunities to attract qualified candidates and build a winning and compassionate team.

Thought Leadership and Brand Building: By sharing industry insights, research findings, success stories, and thought leadership content on LinkedIn, your clinic can establish itself as a leader in the field and enhance its brand reputation. This can attract clients seeking mental health services and professionals looking to work with reputable clinics.

Networking and Collaboration Opportunities: LinkedIn's networking capabilities allow mental health clinics to connect with other healthcare professionals, organizations, and industry influencers. This opens up opportunities for collaborations, partnerships, and referral networks that can benefit the clinic's growth and reach within the mental health community.

Recruitment and Employee Engagement: LinkedIn serves as a platform for showcasing job opportunities, attracting talent, and engaging with current and potential employees. You can use LinkedIn to promote your workplace culture, share employee testimonials, and highlight career development opportunities, fostering employee engagement and retention.

Cons of LinkedIn:

Professional Tone and Content: LinkedIn is a professional networking platform where users expect to engage with industry-related content and discussions. Therefore, it is critical to maintain a professional tone in your marketing efforts on LinkedIn, which may require adapting content to suit the platform's business-focused audience or creating platform-specific content.

Compliance and Privacy Concerns: Ensuring compliance with HIPAA privacy laws and maintaining patient confidentiality can be challenging in a professional networking environment.

Audience Targeting Limitations: While LinkedIn offers robust audience targeting capabilities, the platform's user base may be more limited than that of other social media platforms. Marketing on LinkedIn should be more focused on developing professional relationships, partnerships, and recruiting.

Negative Reactions or Stigma: Discussing mental health topics on a professional platform like LinkedIn may elicit varied reactions from users, ranging from support and engagement to potential stigma or misconceptions about mental health issues. Practices must be prepared to address negative reactions and promote accurate information and understanding about behavioral health. This is a huge opportunity to be an active part of the discussion about mental health awareness, but it will be a commitment.

Resource Allocation and Engagement: Maintaining an active and engaging presence on LinkedIn requires dedicated time and resources to create and share valuable content, engage with followers, and participate in professional discussions. So, you must be willing to allocate resources effectively to manage your LinkedIn presence and maximize engagement.

Personal Branding Focus: While company pages have grown in popularity in recent years, LinkedIn is primarily focused on professional profiles above company pages. This results in professionals needing to commit to posting, commenting, and responding through their own professional accounts over the company pages.

While LinkedIn can be a valuable platform for marketing your practice, it is essential to navigate these potential cons carefully, uphold professional standards, ensure compliance with regulations, and engage with users effectively to leverage the platform's benefits while mitigating risks.

Overall, marketing on LinkedIn offers mental and behavioral health clinics a strategic platform to recruit top talent, build industry authority, and foster valuable professional connections within the healthcare sector. This results in a different focus that makes LinkedIn unique among other social media platforms.

Snapchat

Snapchat is a popular multimedia messaging app known for disappearing messages, filters, lenses, and Stories. Users can send photos, videos, and messages that disappear after being viewed, making the app ideal for sharing ephemeral content. Snapchat's filters and lenses allow users to add fun effects and animations to their photos and videos, enhancing creativity and engagement. Stories enable users to share a series of photos and videos that disappear after 24 hours, creating a real-time and authentic storytelling experience. With a predominantly younger user base, Snapchat has become a platform for personal communication, content creation, and social interaction through visual and interactive content.

While Snapchat offers marketing benefits such as reaching a younger audience and leveraging engaging content formats, it presents unique challenges for those in the mental or medical fields. The platform's high engagement rates come at a cost. Producing the volume of content necessary to effectively reach audiences can be time-consuming, which can be a significant hurdle for most mental or behavioral health practices to overcome.

The decision to invest time into Snapchat is a highly specialized one, depending on your clinic's specialty, patient clientele, and willingness to embrace the exciting challenges of new technology. There are some specialties in the medical fields that are using it effectively, including sports medicine, plastic surgery, OB/GYN, maternity or infertility, and orthodontics. If you are interested or have someone in your office who wants to try out Snapchat as part of your marketing efforts, carefully think through your editorial calendar and plan out your storytelling to be effective. As always, ensure that the material you share complies with HIPAA regulations.

Tiktok

What is TikTok? It is a popular social media platform that allows users to create, share, and discover short-form videos set to music or audio clips. With a focus on creativity, entertainment, and user-generated content, TikTok offers a diverse range of videos spanning comedy, dance, challenges, educational content, and more. The platform's algorithm-driven "For You" page suggests personalized content to users based on their interests and interactions, making it easy to discover new and engaging videos from a global community of creators.

What sets TikTok apart is its user-friendly interface, powerful editing tools, and the ability to turn any content into a viral trend. These unique features have contributed to its rapid growth and appeal among a wide range of users, from influencers and brands to everyday creators looking to share their creativity with a large and engaged audience.

Marketing on TikTok can offer several benefits for mental health marketing efforts, providing a unique and engaging platform to reach a diverse audience and promote mental wellness resources. With its emphasis on creativity and storytelling, TikTok allows you to share educational content, self-care tips, coping strategies, and inspirational messages in a visually compelling and relatable format that resonates with users, fosters community engagement, and destigmatizes conversations around mental health. The platform's algorithm-driven content discovery and viral trends offer opportunities for mental health campaigns to reach a broader audience, increase visibility, and generate user engagement. Overall, marketing on TikTok can help mental health initiatives raise awareness, provide valuable resources, and promote positive mental well-being in a creative and accessible way.

The benefits of marketing on TikTok include reaching a highly engaged and diverse audience, leveraging the platform's algorithm to increase content visibility, and utilizing creative and interactive content formats to drive brand awareness and engagement. TikTok's unique features, such as trending challenges and user-generated content, also provide opportunities for brands to connect with users in an authentic and impactful way.

However, there are significant challenges that you must navigate to effectively promote your clinic's services and resources on the platform. One key challenge is the limited targeting options on TikTok's advertising platform, making it challenging to reach specific audiences interested in mental health resources and support. Additionally, brand safety concerns related to data privacy and content moderation issues on TikTok may raise apprehensions for mental health businesses regarding the platform's suitability for promoting sensitive content. These challenges and the time-consuming nature of creating and curating engaging content for TikTok create hurdles for businesses, requiring significant resources and effort to stay relevant and capture users' attention. Finally, measuring the return on investment (ROI) of marketing efforts on TikTok can be uncertain, as success on the platform is often based on engagement and virality rather than direct conversions, making it challenging for mental health businesses to assess the impact of their marketing campaigns accurately.

Due to the heightened security and HIPAA concerns, in addition to the intense time demands of being effective on TikTok, many mental and behavioral clinics chose to invest their time in other social media channels. Despite these challenges, with strategic planning, creativity, and a deep awareness of the risk involved with using TikTok, some mental and behavioral health clinics have succeeded with the platform.

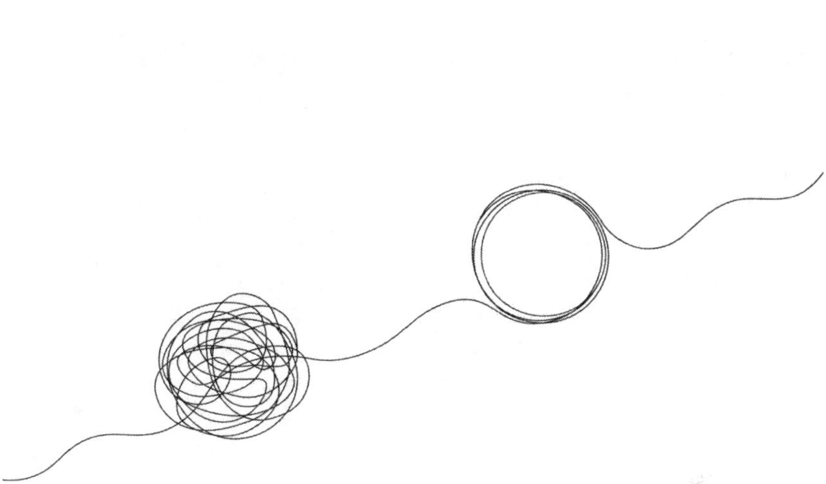

Chapter 7: Paid Ads (PPC)

Paid ads, also known as Pay-Per-Click (PPC) advertising, is where you pay a fee each time one of the ads you've designed and published is clicked. PPC ads are typically displayed on search engine results pages, social media platforms, and other websites, targeting specific keywords or demographics to reach potential customers. The cost of each click is determined through a bidding process, with advertisers setting a maximum bid for their chosen keywords. PPC is valued for its ability to drive immediate traffic, measure performance through detailed analytics, and offer a high degree of control over budget and targeting. Let's dig into the various paid ad platforms and the pros and cons of each.

Paid Ads or PPC are valued for their ability to drive immediate traffic that converts at a high rate.

Facebook (Meta) Ads

Facebook ads offer numerous marketing benefits for mental and behavioral health practices, primarily the ability to target specific audiences based on demographics, interests, and behaviors, ensuring that the ads reach individuals who are likely to be interested in mental health services. Additionally, Facebook's advanced targeting capabilities allow practices to reach potential patients in their local area, increasing the likelihood of converting ad viewers into clients. Facebook ads provide a cost-effective way to promote services and increase brand awareness, as practices can set their own budget and monitor the performance of their ads in real-time. Overall, utilizing Facebook ads can help mental and behavioral health practices attract new clients and expand their reach in a highly targeted and measurable way.

Reach a Targeted Audience

By leveraging Facebook's sophisticated targeting capabilities, you can ensure your ads are seen by the people most likely to be interested in your facility's services. You can target your ads based on demographics such as age, gender, income, location, and language. You can also target people based on their interests, such as hobbies, activities, and pages they've liked, as well as their behaviors, such as purchasing habits and device usage.

This level of precision in targeting is a game-changer for clinics seeking to connect with their ideal clients. By honing in on your audience, you can be certain that your ads are reaching individuals genuinely interested in your offerings. This not only boosts the likelihood of conversions but also saves you money by minimizing wasted ad spend.

Variety of Ad Formats

Facebook ads are highly effective because they offer a wide variety of ad formats. This allows you to tailor ads to your facility's specific marketing objectives and target audience, ensuring that they deliver the most engaging and effective message possible.

One of the most popular ad formats is the **single-image ad**. These ads are simple yet effective, featuring a single image accompanied by a headline, text, and a call to action. They are versatile and can be used to promote a variety of products or services, making them a great option for businesses of all sizes and industries.

For those seeking to elevate their advertising game, **video ads** are a compelling option. They can captivate audiences with product displays, service highlights, or brand narratives, making conversions more likely.

Carousel ads are a popular choice for facilities looking to feature multiple services within one ad. Users can swipe through a series of images or videos, making them ideal when you want to highlight multiple therapists or services.

Slideshow ads are akin to carousel ads but with a more automated touch. They play a sequence of images or videos, engaging your audience with a visually compelling and dynamic ad experience.

Detailed Targeting Options

Facebook's strength is its user base and targeting capabilities. Marketers can combine different targeting parameters to ensure that their ads are seen by the people who are most likely to be interested in their message.

Demographics, including age, gender, education level, job title, and household income, are the basic building blocks of audience segmentation. But you can also use what people are interested in, such as the Pages they like, the apps and ads they click on, and similar types of information, as well as their purchase behaviors, device usage, and other activities.

Facebook also allows you to target people who have already interacted with your business, such as those who have visited your website or engaged with your Facebook page. By targeting these warm leads, you can nurture your relationships and convert them into clients.

Custom audiences, created by uploading customer data such as email lists or CRM data, take targeting to a whole new level. This approach allows clinics to reach individuals who are already familiar with your brand, increasing the likelihood of conversions.

Facebook's lookalike audiences, which identify users who share similar characteristics with existing customers, further extend the reach of targeted advertising. These options are available but must be used carefully only when full compliance with HIPAA regulations is possible.

Moreover, Facebook offers the ability to exclude certain segments from ad campaigns. This means you can prevent your ads from being shown to people who have already seen them or taken a specific action, such as visiting your website. This level of control can help you minimize ad fatigue and make sure your ad dollars go further.

Budget Flexibility

Unlike traditional advertising methods, where businesses are often locked into long-term contracts or expensive ad placements, Facebook ads allow you to set daily or lifetime budget limits that align with your marketing goals and financial resources. This means you have complete control over how much you spend on your ad campaigns, ensuring that you never overextend your budget.

In addition to budget limits, Facebook ads offer granular control over your ad spend through bid caps. With bid caps, you can set the maximum amount you're willing to pay for each ad click or impression. This feature empowers you to optimize your ad spend and ensures that you're only paying for the results you want.

Facebook ads also provide the flexibility to adjust your budget at any time, giving you the agility you need to manage your ad campaigns effectively. If you see positive results and want to invest more, you can increase your budget to reach a larger audience. And if you need to scale back, you can decrease your budget without penalty. This flexibility means you can adapt your ad campaigns to changing market conditions or business priorities.

Measurable Results

One of the most important benefits of Facebook advertising is its ability to provide measurable results. By using Facebook's robust analytics platform, you can gain valuable insights into the performance of your ad campaigns and use that data to make more informed decisions about their advertising strategies.

Facebook offers a range of metrics to help you understand how your ads are performing. These include reach, impressions, clicks, conversions, and more. By monitoring these metrics, you can learn how many people saw your ads, how many times your ads were displayed, how many people clicked on your ads, and how many of those clicks led to a desired action, such as a purchase, sign-up, or app download. This information can help you evaluate the effectiveness of your ad campaigns and make data-driven improvements. For more specific information on what these metrics mean, check out this article by Facebook: https://bit.ly/4enblnu

This level of precision in tracking and measuring conversions allows you to optimize your campaigns in alignment with your business goals and gives you the tools you need to optimize your ad campaigns and achieve your marketing goals more effectively.

Pros and Cons of Facebook Paid Ads

The benefits of Facebook paid ads are numerous and can greatly contribute to your business's success. One of the key advantages of Facebook ads is their ability to reach a large audience quickly and efficiently. With over 2.9 billion monthly active users, Facebook provides businesses with a massive potential customer base. By using the platform's extensive reach, businesses can greatly increase their visibility and attract a larger audience, which can lead to more leads and conversions.

Moreover, Facebook paid ads offer unparalleled targeting. Businesses can pinpoint their audience based on demographics, interests, behaviors, and even keywords. This precision ensures that ads are shown to individuals who are most likely to be interested in the products or services being offered, thus maximizing the effectiveness of ad campaigns and minimizing wasted ad spend.

Furthermore, Facebook paid ads offer businesses financial control, enabling them to set and manage their advertising budget. Whether it's a daily or lifetime budget, businesses can rest assured they won't exceed their financial limits. This is especially advantageous for small businesses or those with more modest marketing resources, allowing them to maintain a strong grip on their advertising costs while still reaching their target audience.

Facebook paid ads also offer a wealth of insights and analytics through their powerful tracking and reporting features. You can monitor the performance of your ad campaigns in real-time, tracking metrics like impressions, clicks, conversions, and engagement. This data allows you to evaluate the effectiveness of your ads, pinpoint areas for enhancement, and optimize your campaigns for superior results.

If you are looking for a step-by-step tutorial for getting started with Facebook ads, check out this article: https://bit.ly/4dXDwtt

All in all, Facebook is a premium channel for paid ads for mental and behavioral health facilities. That being said, there are also some challenges that must be aware of. One challenge is the strict advertising policies and regulations that Facebook has in place for healthcare-related ads. These policies can make it difficult for clinics to create ads that comply with Facebook's guidelines, resulting in ads being rejected or disapproved. There are limitations on the types of services or treatments that clinics can advertise, which can restrict the effectiveness of their PPC campaigns. For more information on what Facebook's limitations are, check out this article: https://bit.ly/3MIUxvh

Some of the limitations include:

Prohibited content: Facebook prohibits ads that promote the use of certain mental health-related products or services, such as prescription medications, tobacco, and illegal drugs.

Sensitive content: Ads related to sensitive mental health topics, such as suicide, self-harm, or eating disorders, are subject to additional scrutiny and may be restricted or disapproved.

Targeting restrictions: Facebook limits the ability to target certain demographics, such as age, gender, or interests, when it comes to ads related to mental health. This is to prevent discrimination or targeting vulnerable populations.

Misleading claims: Facebook does not allow ads that make false or misleading claims about mental health treatments or services.

Community standards: Ads that violate Facebook's community standards, such as promoting violence, hate speech, or discrimination, are strictly prohibited, including those related to mental health.

Mental health clinics must carefully review and comply with Facebook's advertising policies and guidelines to ensure their ads are approved and reach their intended audience effectively.

Google Ads

Google Ads is an online advertising platform developed by Google that allows businesses to create and display ads on Google's search engine results pages and other Google properties. Advertisers (you) bid on keywords relevant to your clinic's services to have your ads displayed to users who are searching for those keywords. The ads can appear at the top or bottom of search results pages, as well as on websites within the Google Display Network. You pay for your ads based on a pay-per-click (PPC) model, meaning you only pay when a user clicks on your ad.

Google Ads uses a combination of bid amount, ad quality, and relevance to determine ad placement and ad rank, with the goal of providing users with relevant and useful ads. Google Ads allows you to connect with those actively seeking mental health and well-being services. By targeting these specific searches, your ads are more likely to be seen by those who are genuinely interested in your clinic, increasing the potential for higher-quality leads.

Refine your targeting even further by narrowing your audience based on specific criteria. With Google Ads, you can define your target audience by location, ensuring that your ads are shown to people in your desired geographic area. You can also target your ads based on demographics, interests, and even specific life events. This level of targeting can help you reach the right people at the right time and increase your chances of making a connection with someone who needs your services.

Elevate your ad's impact with ad extensions. These additional snippets of information can include your services, location, and contact details, making your ad more comprehensive and compelling. By incorporating ad extensions, you increase the likelihood of users engaging with your ad and taking the next step to visit your website or get in touch with your clinic.

Another way to build trust and credibility with potential clients is by using reviews and other forms of social proof in your ads. By displaying positive reviews and testimonials from satisfied clients, you can show the effectiveness of your services. Social proof can be a powerful endorsement, influencing how users perceive your clinic and encouraging them to choose your services over others.

Create compelling ad copy that speaks directly to your target audience. Use language that resonates with their needs, concerns, and aspirations. Highlight the unique benefits of your clinic and the positive impact your services can have on their lives. By optimizing your ad copy, you can increase its click-through rate and drive more qualified traffic to your website.

For addiction recovery treatment centers, it's important to note that you must be LegitScript-certified to advertise on Google. LegitScript (https://www.legitscript.com) is a third-party certification service that helps healthcare providers meet regulatory requirements and ensures your ads comply with Google's advertising policies. For more information on Legit Script, check out this article. https://bit.ly/4gmLSfw

Advanced targeting options

With Google Ads, mental and behavioral health clinics can embark on a targeted advertising journey, ensuring their messages reach those in need at the opportune moment. With intentionally crafted targeting options, clinics can connect with individuals actively seeking the services they offer. By aligning your ads with relevant keywords, phrases, and topics related to mental health and well-being, you can enhance your chances of captivating higher-quality leads.

Google Ads allows clinics to target individuals with great precision, taking into account their location, demographics, and interests. This granular targeting approach lets you tailor your campaigns to specific segments of the population. For example, you can target people in a certain geographic area to make sure your ads are seen by those close to your clinic. They can also use targeting options based on age, gender, and life events, such as a recent divorce or job loss, to reach people who may need mental health support.

Remarketing, a key feature of Google Ads, takes targeting to the next level. This powerful tool allows clinics to connect with people who have previously visited your website. By showing these people relevant ads across the web or when they search on Google, you can increase the likelihood that they'll become patients. For example, you can show ads to people who visited your services page, read a blog post, or downloaded a resource. This way, you can bring people back to your site and keep your clinic at the top of their minds when they're ready to get help.

With Google Ads, mental and behavioral health clinics can run targeted advertising campaigns that reach the right people at the right time. By using advanced targeting options, you can connect with people who are more likely to be interested in your services. This can lead to a higher return on investment and a healthier, happier community. Targeted advertising can help clinics like yours fulfill their mission of providing timely, accessible mental healthcare to those who need it most.

Measurable Results

With Google Ads, mental and behavioral health facilities can track and measure the success of their online advertising. Real-time tracking and performance metrics provide valuable insights into ad performance, allowing you to make informed decisions and optimize your campaigns. You can see how many people see your ads, visit your website, or call your clinic. Then, use this data to improve your campaigns and allocate your budget more effectively.

Moreover, the integration with Google Analytics empowers clinics to delve into user behavior on their websites, identifying trends, preferences, and areas for enhancement. Armed with this comprehensive understanding, you can personalize your Google Ads campaigns and website content to better resonate with your target audience.

The A/B testing feature in Google Ads is another powerful tool that can help you optimize your ad campaigns and get the most out of your ad budget. By testing different ad variations, such as ad copy, images, and landing pages, you can see which ones resonate with your target audience and drive the most conversions. This data-driven approach can help you make sure you're using the most effective ad strategies and getting the best results from your Google Ads campaigns.

Budget Control

A pivotal advantage of Google Ads for mental and behavioral health clinics is the ability to manage advertising budgets with precision. Unlike the unpredictability of traditional advertising costs, Google Ads offers meticulous control over daily and lifetime budgets. This flexibility allows you to establish spending limits that are in harmony with your financial goals, preventing overspending.

Google Ads equips you with the power to **fine-tune your bids** and budgets in response to your campaign's performance. This dynamic feature allows you to optimize your ad spend by directing more resources to successful campaigns and scaling back on those that aren't delivering. By diligently monitoring and analyzing your campaign data, you can make informed adjustments to maximize your return on investment. Features like **optimized ad delivery** ensure that your ads are shown when they're most likely to be clicked, reducing wasted impressions and maximizing your budget. **Automated bidding strategies**, including target CPA (cost per action) and target ROAS (return on ad spend), can streamline your budget management by adjusting bids to meet your performance objectives.

By taking advantage of these budget control features, you can effectively manage your advertising expenses and achieve your desired results. Google Ads empowers you to allocate your financial resources wisely, optimize ad performance, and ultimately reach your target audience while staying within your budget limits.

Flexible Ad Formats

Google Ads formats are designed to fit the unique needs of your mental and behavioral health clinic. With **responsive ads**, you can create an ad that automatically adjusts its size, look, and format to fit just about any available ad space. Fill in your ad text, images, and URL, and let Google Ads do the rest.

For mental and behavioral health clinics looking to drive immediate action, **call-only ads** offer a direct line of communication. They include a clickable "call" button, making it easy for people to call your clinic directly from search results. Remove barriers and make it easier for potential clients to take the most important step toward care.

Harness the emotional power of **video ads** to create a deep connection with your audience. Share inspiring patient testimonials that show the life-changing impact of your services. Educate and demonstrate your treatment methods to build trust and position your clinic as a place of hope and expertise. Video ads make a lasting, positive impression, helping you promote your clinic and connect with potential clients.

Use the flexibility of Google Ads' range of ad formats to reach your audience across devices and deliver messages that resonate. By being there with the right message at the right time, you can help drive meaningful results for your clinic. And, with the flexibility to change your campaign settings at any time, you can work towards your goals and make a positive impact on the lives of people who need your services.

Instagram

Instagram serves as a powerful platform for expanding your audience, generating leads, and increasing awareness surrounding mental health issues. With its highly interactive user base and advanced targeting features, paid ads on Instagram offer a unique opportunity to connect with individuals who may benefit from your services. By crafting compelling ad copy that resonates with your target audience, pinpointing the right demographics and interests to target, establishing a budget that aligns with your marketing objectives, and closely monitoring and interpreting your campaign outcomes, you can leverage Instagram paid ads to effectively engage with potential clients and drive meaningful results. Embracing this strategic approach to marketing on Instagram can not only elevate your brand visibility but also foster meaningful connections with individuals seeking mental health support, ultimately contributing to the growth and success of your facility.

Write Compelling Ad Copy

With Instagram paid ads, your ad copy is key to capturing your audience's attention and compelling them to act. Here are some tips to help you write compelling copy that drives results:

Begin with a compelling message. Your ad copy must seize the audience's attention from the start and deliver your message clearly and succinctly. Avoid jargon or technical terms that might alienate your potential clients. Instead, opt for straightforward language that resonates with their desires and concerns.

Emphasize the distinctive advantages of your clinicians and service. What sets your offering apart from the rest? Ensure your ad copy highlights these unique benefits. Articulate how your offering can resolve an issue or provide a solution for your target audience.

Incorporate relevant keywords. When crafting your ad copy, be sure to incorporate relevant keywords that your target audience is likely to use when searching for facilities or services like yours. This will help your ad appear in more relevant search results and increase its visibility.

Employ a compelling call to action (CTA). Your ad copy must feature a robust CTA that motivates users to act as you desire, whether it's visiting your website, downloading a resource, or booking an appointment. Ensure your CTA is unmistakable, precise, and easily acted upon.

Experiment with different ad copy. Don't shy away from testing various ad copy to find what resonates best with your audience. Instagram's ad platform is designed to make this process easy, enabling you to optimize your ad copy for maximum impact.

By adhering to these guidelines, you can craft Instagram paid ad copy that seizes attention, underscores your unique benefits, and compels the actions you seek from your audience. Keep in mind that your ad copy often serves as the initial introduction of your brand to potential clients—make it count.

Utilize High-quality Images and Videos.

High-quality images and videos are a must for your Instagram paid ads to be effective. When selecting visuals, make sure they are relevant to your target audience and showcase your facility's services and practitioners in the best way possible. Use images that will catch your audience's attention and are clear, easy to understand, and consistent with your brand.

Videos are a great way to make your ad more engaging. They can help you show how your program works, and they can add a personal touch to your brand. Keep your videos short and sweet, and make sure to get your message across in the first few seconds to keep people watching. Don't stress too much about being perfect! Having content out there is better than nothing at all. Make sure the topics and information in your video ads are HIPAA compliant and have fun with it. Your audience won't respond to overly produced videos, so be real, be raw, and connect with your audience.

Don't stress too much about being perfect! Having content out there is better than nothing at all.

Remember, Instagram is a mobile-first platform, so optimizing your images and videos for mobile is key. Make sure your visuals look good on a small screen, and use a vertical format to match how people naturally scroll through their feeds. By keeping these best practices in mind, you can create Instagram ads that are visually compelling, drive great results, and help you achieve your business goals.

Target the Right Audience

Targeting the right audience is crucial for the success of your Instagram paid ads. This goes back to the conversation we had with the target audience in every section. Leverage the profiles you have made and make sure your ads are connecting with potential client's needs, wants, and pain points. Meet them where they are at. There are several ways to use the information in your target audience profile to define your ads on Instagram:

Demographics: Instagram lets you target many demographics, including age, gender, and more. Tailoring your ad content and messaging to these specifics will help you connect with your ideal customers.

Interests: Instagram also allows users to be targeted based on their interests, including hobbies, activities, and favorite brands. This information can be leveraged to create highly relevant ad campaigns that resonate with your target audience.

In mental or behavioral health marketing on Instagram, targeting users based on their behaviors is key. By analyzing purchasing habits, website visits, and app usage, you can connect with individuals already engaged with your services or those likely to be interested. This data-driven approach enhances your outreach and engagement strategies.

For even more precise targeting, **Instagram provides audience insights** that offer a wealth of data on demographics, interests, and behaviors. This information empowers you to craft highly personalized and impactful ad campaigns. You can craft custom audiences from your website visitors, email lists, or CRM data, reaching out to those who have already engaged with your brand or are existing customers.

Lastly, **lookalike audiences** are a powerful tool to connect with individuals who resemble your current customer base. Instagram's algorithm scrutinizes the characteristics of your existing customers and identifies users with similar traits. This is an effective way to broaden your reach and engage new customers who are likely to be interested in what you offer.

By refining your targeting based on location, language, or device, you can heighten the relevance of your ads and ensure they reach the right audience. This precision in targeting empowers you to optimize your ad spend and maximize the return on your investment.

Set a Budget and Bidding Strategy

When you set up your Instagram paid ad campaign, you'll have the option to choose a daily budget or a lifetime budget. The daily budget is the maximum you're willing to spend per day, while the lifetime budget is the maximum you're willing to spend during the lifetime of your ad campaign. Sticking to your budget is the best way to avoid overspending and manage your ad campaign effectively.

Equally important is selecting the right bidding strategy. Instagram offers a variety of bidding strategies, each designed to help you achieve a specific goal with your ad. For example, the 'Cost per Click' (CPC) strategy charges you when someone clicks on your ad, which can be a good option for driving people to your website. The 'Cost per Mille' (CPM) strategy charges you based on 1,000 impressions, which can be a good option for when you want to build brand awareness.

When you set your bid, you're telling Instagram how much you're willing to pay to have your ad shown or clicked on. You can choose between a manual bid or an automatic bid. With a manual bid, you set the maximum amount you're willing to pay. With an automatic bid, Instagram will set your bid to help you get the most engagement within your budget.

Bid modifiers are powerful tools that allow you to adjust your bids based on specific criteria, such as device type, location, and time of day. This can help you focus your ad spend on the most relevant audience and optimize your ad performance.

Last but not least, regular monitoring and analysis of your campaign's performance are crucial. Instagram offers insights into your ad's performance, from impressions to clicks and conversions. This data empowers you to evaluate the effectiveness of your campaign and make the necessary adjustments to your budget and bidding strategy. By setting your budget and bidding strategy thoughtfully and analyzing your results, you can greatly enhance your chances of success with Instagram paid ads.

Monitor and Analyze your Results

Monitoring and analyzing the performance of your Instagram paid ads is crucial to determining their effectiveness and making informed optimizations. Instagram Insights, a built-in analytics tool, provides valuable data to help you evaluate your ad campaigns.

Key metrics to monitor include reach, impressions, engagement, and click-through rates. Reach measures the number of unique users who saw your ad, while impressions count the number of times your ad was displayed. Engagement metrics, such as likes, comments, and shares, indicate how your audience interacts with your ad. Click-through rates measure how many users clicked on your ad and were directed to your website or landing page.

Delving into your audience's demographics and behaviors can yield valuable insights into who is most receptive to your ads. This information can help you fine-tune your targeting and craft more compelling ads for your desired audience. A/B testing is a potent strategy for optimizing your Instagram paid ads. By crafting multiple ad variations with distinct elements—such as ad copy, images, or calls to action—you can pinpoint what resonates most with your audience. Instagram's integrated split testing feature streamlines the process, enabling you to identify the most effective ad with ease.

Last but not least, tracking your return on investment (ROI) is crucial for gauging the financial success of your Instagram ad campaign. Calculate your ROI by dividing the revenue generated from your ad campaign by the total amount you spent on advertising. This metric will help you ascertain if your ad campaign is yielding a positive return and meeting your business objectives.

Regular monitoring and analysis of your Instagram paid ads performance will enable you to make data-driven decisions, optimize your campaigns, and maximize your return on investment. By embracing these analytics tools and strategies, you can ensure your Instagram paid ads deliver the desired results and contribute to your business growth.

YouTube

Welcome to the world of YouTube advertising! This section is all about helping you understand the benefits and drawbacks and how to make the most of the platform. We'll cover how to target your audience, choose the right ad format, set your budget and bidding strategy, create compelling ad content, and track and analyze your results.

Pros of YouTube

The biggest advantage of YouTube ads is their reach. With 2 billion monthly active users, YouTube is one of the most visited websites online. This gives you the opportunity to reach a massive audience to help you tap into new markets, increase brand awareness, and drive traffic to your websites.

The biggest advantage of YouTube ads is their reach. With 2 billion monthly active users, YouTube is one of the most visited websites online.

What's more, YouTube's advanced targeting options allow you to zero in on your ideal audience. As with all of the social media platforms, you can target by age, gender, location, interests, and even by the keywords and phrases your audience is likely to use. Ideally, this means you can ensure your ads are seen by the people who are most likely to want your products or services, which will ultimately help you get better results from your ad spend.

With YouTube ads, you also have control over your budget. You can set a daily budget for your ad campaigns, which means you won't overspend. You can also adjust your budget at any time based on your performance and campaign goals.

YouTube also provides a suite of analytics tools to help you track and analyze the performance of your ad campaigns. You can get detailed insights into audience engagement, views, watch time, and more. These tools can help you understand how your audience is responding to your ads and how you can improve your campaigns to get better results.

Cons of YouTube

One significant hurdle is the cost. YouTube ads can be pricier than those on other platforms, particularly for competitive industries or specific demographics. Before launching a YouTube advertising campaign, you must carefully assess the budget and balance the potential costs against the expected benefits.

Another hurdle is the intense competition on YouTube. With millions of creators and businesses vying for attention, it can be difficult for ads to stand out and capture viewers' interest. Creating high-quality, engaging, and visually appealing ad content becomes paramount to cutting through the noise and effectively conveying the brand's message.

The final challenge is that ad-blocking software can prevent ads from being displayed to users, limiting the reach and effectiveness of ad campaigns. When evaluating the potential impact of ad performance, businesses should take into account that some users may use ad-blocking software.

In summary, YouTube advertising is a robust tool for reaching a wide audience, honing in on your target market, managing your budget, and monitoring your success. However, it's important to be aware of the potential costs, competition, and ad-blocking challenges that come with the territory. By taking these factors into account and implementing effective strategies, you can unlock the full potential of YouTube ads and drive growth for your business.

Targeting Your Audience

One of the cornerstones of a successful YouTube advertising campaign is the precision with which you target your audience. YouTube provides a range of options to ensure that your message reaches those most likely to engage with your product or service. These options include:

Demographic targeting: Target your audience by age, gender, and parental status. This is a powerful tool for reaching specific groups, such as young parents or the millennial generation.

Interest targeting allows you to target your ads to people with specific interests, such as travel, fashion, or technology.

Remarketing: This feature enables you to re-engage with those who have previously visited your website or interacted with your brand. It's a powerful tool for reinforcing your message and prompting action.

Keyword targeting: Reach potential customers based on the keywords they're searching for. This can be a great way to get in front of people who are looking for help and need the services your facility can provide.

Placement targeting: allows you to direct your ads to particular videos, channels, or websites. This is a powerful tool for reaching an audience interested in specific content or already engaged with your brand.

Choosing the Right Ad Format

YouTube offers a variety of ad formats to help you achieve your marketing goals. To help you choose the right format, we'll take a closer look at the different ad formats available on YouTube and the best practices for using each one.

Skippable vs. Non-skippable Ads: Skippable ads allow viewers to skip after five seconds, while non-skippable ads must be watched in their entirety. Skippable ads are typically shorter, cost-effective, and can generate higher viewership. However, non-skippable ads provide guaranteed impressions and higher engagement rates.

In-Stream Ads vs. Display Ads: In-stream ads play before, during, or after other videos, while display ads appear alongside related videos or on the YouTube search results page. In-stream ads offer a more immersive experience and higher engagement, while display ads are more cost-effective and can drive website traffic.

Video Ads vs. Image Ads: Video ads are the most common format, allowing you to showcase your product or service visually. Image ads, on the other hand, are static and often used for branding purposes or to promote events. Video ads are more engaging and memorable, but image ads can be more cost-effective.

Companion Banners: These small, rectangular ads can be displayed alongside video ads. They provide additional information or a call to action and can increase click-through rates.

Regardless of the ad format you select, it is crucial to include a clear call to action (CTA) to encourage viewers to take the desired action, such as visiting your website, subscribing to your channel, or making a purchase. An effective CTA should be brief, specific, and create a sense of urgency.

By carefully considering the available ad formats and tailoring your choice to your campaign goals, you can optimize your YouTube advertising strategy for maximum impact and conversions.

Setting your Budget and Bidding Strategy

Determining your budget is a key part of setting up your YouTube ad campaign. Start by thinking about how much you want to spend for the month. Factors like your business goals, target audience, and the content you're advertising against can all influence what you should spend. YouTube allows you to set a daily budget, which means the average amount you're willing to spend each day, or a lifetime budget, which is the total amount you're willing to spend over the duration of your campaign.

Selecting the appropriate bidding strategy is crucial for maximizing your ad spend and reaching your campaign goals. YouTube provides a variety of bidding strategies, each designed for specific objectives. If you want to drive website traffic or conversions, you can use Cost-Per-Action (CPA) bidding. With CPA bidding, you pay only when viewers take a specific action, such as clicking on your ad and visiting your website.

On the other hand, if you want to maximize your ad's visibility and reach, you can choose Cost-Per-View (CPV) bidding. With CPV bidding, you pay each time your ad is viewed for at least 30 seconds or when a user interacts with it, whichever comes first. For maximum control over your ad spend, you can set your maximum bid amount, which represents the highest amount you're willing to pay for a click or view. This allows you to stay within your budget while still ensuring your ad remains competitive in the auction.

As always, monitoring your campaign's performance is essential to ensure you're maximizing the value of your YouTube ad investment. YouTube offers robust analytics that let you track metrics like impressions, clicks, views, and conversions. By analyzing this data, you can see what's resonating with your audience and what's not and make informed adjustments to your budget and bidding strategy.

Creating High-Quality Ad Content

When it comes to YouTube advertising, creating high-quality ad content is key to the success of your campaign. Your ads should be relevant to your target audience and tailored to their interests, effectively conveying your message and prompting them to take action.

To do this, start with your target audience research and profiles from Chapter 2 to understand their preferences, pain points, and motivations. This will help you create an ad that feels personal to them. Make sure your ad is also concise and attention-grabbing, capturing the viewer's interest within the first few seconds. A strong hook, compelling visuals, and a clear call to action are all important for this.

Furthermore, the power of storytelling can be harnessed to create an emotional connection with your audience. A compelling narrative can be shared, demonstrating how your clinicians and facility can address their needs and enrich their lives. This approach will render your ad more memorable and increase the likelihood of your audience taking the desired action. Always remember, your ad should not only inform but also inspire and engage your audience. It goes without saying that you should ensure any storytelling or ads are HIPAA compliant in their visuals and messaging.

When it comes to visuals, make sure they are high-quality, relevant, and eye-catching.

When it comes to visuals, make sure they are high-quality, relevant, and eye-catching. Use visually appealing images, animations, or videos that are consistent with your brand and resonate with your target audience. Similarly, your audio should be clear, engaging, and synchronized with the visuals.

Last but not least, optimize your ad for mobile. A large portion of YouTube watch time comes from mobile devices, so it's important to make sure your ad is viewable and easy to interact with on small screens.

Tracking and Analyzing Your Results

Tracking and analyzing the performance of your YouTube ad campaigns is crucial for measuring their success and making data-driven optimizations. **YouTube Analytics**, a powerful tool provided by YouTube, offers comprehensive insights into your campaign's effectiveness. By utilizing YouTube Analytics, you can monitor key metrics such as impressions, clicks, views, and conversions, providing valuable information about your ad's reach and engagement. Additionally, you can gain insights into audience demographics, geographic distribution, and device preferences, enabling you to refine your targeting strategies and optimize your ad creatives.

To take your analysis a step further, consider using A/B testing to compare different ad variations. This method allows you to test different ad elements, such as headlines, descriptions, thumbnails, and targeting options, to see which combination of elements performs the best. A/B testing can help you make more informed decisions and improve your ad campaigns over time.

Tracking conversions is a crucial step in evaluating the overall success of your YouTube ad campaigns. By integrating Google Ads conversion tracking or third-party analytics tools, you can measure valuable actions taken by users after viewing your ads, such as website visits, purchases, or sign-ups. This data enables you to calculate your return on investment (ROI) and determine the true impact of your YouTube advertising efforts.

Regularly reviewing and analyzing your campaign performance is key to making necessary adjustments and achieving optimal results. By closely monitoring your campaign data, you can identify trends, spot opportunities for improvement, and allocate your budget effectively. This data-driven approach ensures that your YouTube ad campaigns are delivering the desired outcomes and driving business growth.

Twitter (X)

Twitter ads can be effective for behavioral or mental health marketing under some specific conditions. Twitter provides a unique opportunity for businesses to connect with their customers. Let's explore the effectiveness of Twitter ads, including the various targeting options, costs, and real-life examples of successful campaigns. We'll also look at the pros and cons of using Twitter ads to help you determine if it's the right fit for your business.

How Twitter Ads Work

Twitter ads seamlessly fit into users' timelines, making them less intrusive and more likely to be seen. Twitter ads can also be displayed in search results, allowing businesses to target users based on their interests and intent. Like Google and Meta, Twitter's advertising platform operates on an auction-based system, which means that the ads that are displayed are based on their relevance and competitiveness. Advertisers bid on specific keywords or user characteristics, and the highest bidders' ads are displayed more prominently. This auction-based approach means that businesses only pay when users engage with their ads.

Similar to the other social media platforms we've looked at, advertisers can pinpoint their audience based on a variety of factors, including location, interests, keywords, and specific behaviors. This precision enables businesses to craft campaigns that reach the right people with remarkable accuracy.

Targeting Options for Twitter Ads

A standout feature of Twitter Ads is the capability to zero in on users by their interests, behavioral targeting, keywords, and locations. This results in heightened engagement, potential conversions, and a more substantial return on investment.

Here are some additional tips for creating effective Twitter Ads:

- Use high-quality images and videos to capture attention and make your ads pop.
- Keep your ad copy concise and pertinent to your audience's needs and interests.
- Employ a clear call to action to direct users to the appropriate steps, such as "Click here to learn more" or "Buy now."

- Keep a watchful eye on your ad campaigns and be ready to make adjustments for better performance.

How much do Twitter ads cost?

Twitter's advertising platform functions on a cost-per-engagement (CPE) or cost-per-click (CPC) model, ensuring that you only pay when users interact with your ads by clicking, retweeting, or liking them.

The cost of Twitter ads is influenced by several factors, including your target audience, budget, and bidding strategy. The more specific your targeting, the more you might pay per engagement. For example, targeting a specific niche with particular interests or demographics could result in a higher cost per engagement than targeting a more general audience.

To manage your Twitter ad expenses, you have the flexibility to set a daily or lifetime budget for each campaign. This feature ensures you remain within your financial limits and prevents overspending. Twitter's bidding system offers a choice between automatic bidding, where Twitter handles the bidding on your behalf, and manual bidding, where you set the maximum bid per engagement.

Twitter also equips you with valuable conversion tracking tools to gauge the efficacy of your ad campaigns. By implementing conversion tracking, you can monitor specific user actions following their interaction with your ads, such as site visits, purchases, or sign-ups. This data-driven approach empowers you to fine-tune your campaigns and optimize your return on investment.

What are some of the Challenges to Marketing on Twitter (X)

The character limit for tweets can be a challenge, requiring clinics to get creative and to the point with their messaging. Additionally, because Twitter's user base skews younger, businesses targeting older demographics might find it difficult to reach their desired audience on the platform. In recent years, people primarily use Twitter to access news and get up-to-date information on events. It is important to keep this in mind when marketing on this platform and keep posts focused on industry trends and helpful information about mental health awareness.

In conclusion, Twitter ads are a great opportunity for facilities looking to increase their reach, drive website traffic, increase mental health awareness, and spread brand awareness. By leveraging Twitter's large user base, cost-effectiveness, easy-to-use platform, and targeting capabilities, businesses can create successful ad campaigns that align with their marketing goals.

LinkedIn

LinkedIn can be a powerful platform for brand credibility and spreading awareness about mental health issues many professionals face. It is the only platform that focuses on professionals in the workplace, and as such, it has a very specialized audience.

Generally speaking, advertising on LinkedIn is the most expensive per capita. This is usually because it is primarily a business-to-business platform. For most mental or behavioral health facilities, recruiting ads result in the best ROI. LinkedIn is most effective as a place to build credibility in your industry and to recruit top talent.

If you are going to experiment with paid ads on LinkedIn, here are some tips:

Choose the right ad format

When you create a LinkedIn ad campaign, choosing the right ad format is a key factor in its success. LinkedIn offers several ad formats, each with its own strengths and purposes. Here, we'll take a look at the several that are particularly effective in recruiting:

Sponsored Content Ads: Sponsored Content ads are designed to appear in the LinkedIn feed and are seamlessly integrated with organic content. They are the perfect vehicle for sharing articles, videos, infographics, and mental health information to build awareness.

Text Ads: LinkedIn's text ads are a straightforward yet powerful ad format that appears on the right side of the desktop interface. They comprise a headline, a brief description, and a call-to-action button and are ideal for prompting swift actions, such as website visits or lead generation. They can also be effectively combined with other ad formats.

Dynamic Ads: Dynamic ads use LinkedIn's user data to craft personalized and highly relevant ad experiences. These ads automatically adjust based on the viewer's profile information, such as job title, industry, or interests. They are the perfect fit for lead-generation campaigns and can notably enhance conversion rates by delivering customized messages to each user.

By thoughtfully choosing the right ad format for your campaign goals and audience, you can elevate the impact of your LinkedIn ad campaigns and reach your business objectives.

Target your Ideal Audience

To ensure your LinkedIn ad campaigns reach the right people and deliver the best results, it's crucial to precisely target your ideal audience. LinkedIn's advanced targeting options enable you to define your target audience based on various criteria, including demographics, job title, industry, skills, and interests. This level of specificity allows you to tailor your ad campaigns to specific segments of your target market, increasing the relevance and effectiveness of your ad messages.

LinkedIn also allows you to target individuals based on their interactions with your company. This includes targeting individuals who have visited your website, engaged with your posts or ads, or are part of your LinkedIn group. This level of targeting enables you to nurture existing relationships and convert warm leads into customers.

Create Compelling Ad Copy

Begin with a powerful hook: Engage your audience immediately with a captivating statement, question, or statistic. This will pique their interest and encourage them to read on.

Keep it short and sweet: Your ad copy should be concise, as there is limited space on LinkedIn. Focus on your key message and the most relevant benefits of your organization and the position.

Employ robust verbs and action words: Infuse your copy with compelling verbs and action words to instill a sense of urgency and inspire your audience to act. For instance, opt for "Apply now" or "Get started today" over a passive "Learn more."

Personalize your ad copy: Tailor your ad copy to the distinct interests and needs of your target audience. Leverage LinkedIn's targeting options to segment your audience and personalize your ad copy. This will make your ads more relevant and engaging, ultimately boosting the likelihood of conversion.

Test different variations: Don't be afraid to experiment with different ad copy variations to see what works best. Try different headlines, descriptions, and calls to action to determine which combination generates the most clicks and conversions. LinkedIn's campaign management platform provides tools for A/B testing, making it easy to compare the performance of different ad copy variations.

It is important to remember that compelling ad copy is the cornerstone of a triumphant LinkedIn ad campaign. By adhering to these guidelines, you can craft ad copy that seizes attention, sparks engagement, and fulfills your business goals.

Set a Budget and Bidding Strategy

Your budget should align with your marketing goals and the resources you have available. You can choose between daily and lifetime budgets, depending on the duration of your campaign and how you want to spend your budget. A daily budget lets you set the maximum amount that you're willing to spend in a day, while a lifetime budget is the total amount you're willing to spend over the duration of your campaign.

Selecting the most appropriate bidding strategy is crucial for the success of your ad campaign. LinkedIn provides a range of bidding options, including Cost-Per-Click (CPC), Cost-Per-Thousand-Impressions (CPM), and Cost-Per-Lead (CPL). CPC ensures you only pay when someone interacts with your ad, making it a great choice for lead generation. CPM is the preferred option for those aiming to boost brand recognition, as you pay for every thousand ad impressions. CPL is used when lead generation is your primary objective, as you only pay when a lead is generated.

After selecting your bidding strategy, you will establish your maximum bid amount. This figure represents the highest sum you are willing to invest for each click, impression, or lead. It is advised to initiate with a conservative bid and then, after evaluating your campaign's efficacy, consider incremental adjustments to optimize your results.

Monitor and Optimize your Ads

Monitoring and optimizing your LinkedIn ad campaigns is crucial to ensuring their effectiveness and achieving your business goals. Review ad performance data, including impressions, clicks, conversions, and engagement metrics, regularly to gain valuable insights into how your ads are performing. Identifying trends and patterns in ad performance allows you to make data-driven adjustments and continuously improve campaign results.

LinkedIn's conversion tracking tool is an essential resource for gauging the success of your ad campaigns and fine-tuning them for better outcomes. By embedding the conversion tracking code on your website or landing page, you can monitor and analyze the specific actions taken by users who engage with your ads, such as form completions, purchases, or other desired outcomes. Armed with this data, you can accurately calculate your return on investment (ROI) and optimize your campaigns to boost conversions and meet your business objectives.

LinkedIn is a powerful marketing platform for building brand awareness, increasing confidence in your organization, and recruiting quality talent for your team. For ads, look to integrate them into your facility's recruitment campaigns, and keep in mind that LinkedIn is primarily a business-to-business (B2B) platform.

Pinterest

Among the many ad platforms available, Pinterest has emerged as a powerful tool for mental or behavioral health clinics looking to engage with a highly visual and receptive audience. In this section, we'll explore the effectiveness of Pinterest ads and provide expert tips and strategies to help you make the most of this platform for successful advertising. We'll cover everything from understanding Pinterest ad basics to targeting the right audience, creating engaging ads, tracking and analyzing performance, and discussing the pros and cons of Pinterest ads. By the end of this post, you'll have a solid understanding of how to use Pinterest ads to drive traffic, generate leads, and achieve your marketing objectives.

Understanding Pinterest Ad Basics

Pinterest ads appear in users' feeds as promoted pins, which are regular pins that you can pay to promote. Each promoted pin features a small "Promoted" label in the top-left corner, so they're easy to spot.

With Pinterest ads, you can precisely target the ideal audience you created earlier in this book based on various factors, including interests, keywords, demographics, and even specific actions taken on the platform. As with other channels, this level of targeting ensures that ads are shown to users who are genuinely interested in the products or services being offered, increasing the likelihood of engagement and conversions.

Pinterest ads can serve a variety of purposes based on your clinic's marketing objectives.

- They can drive traffic to a website, which can result in more valuable visits and increased chances of conversion.
- They can help businesses generate leads by capturing user information through lead generation forms on your website or by encouraging users to take specific actions, such as signing up for a newsletter or booking an appointment.
- They increase brand awareness by helping people discover and save ideas from businesses that they may not have heard of before.

Pinterest ads are also cost-effective. Compared to other advertising platforms, Pinterest ads offer competitive pricing and a high potential for return on investment. You can set daily or lifetime budgets that align with your marketing goals and track your ad performance in real-time to optimize your campaigns for efficiency.

Pinterest ads are a robust tool for businesses to connect with their target audience in a compelling and cost-effective manner. By mastering the fundamentals of Pinterest ads—such as their visual appeal, targeting options, and adaptability to various marketing objectives—businesses can effectively harness this platform to drive traffic, generate leads, boost brand recognition, and ultimately realize their business aspirations.

Targeting the Right Audience

As with every social media ad campaign, the key to successful Pinterest advertising is reaching the right audience. To do this, reference back to your target audience profile from Chapter 2 to identify your ideal customers and what they are interested in.

Pinterest offers a wide range of targeting options, including keywords, phrases, interests, and user lists. By using relevant keywords and phrases, you can help your ads appear in search results when people look for products or services like yours. You can also use eye-catching images and videos to capture people's attention. Since Pinterest is a visual platform, high-quality visuals can help improve your ad performance and increase engagement.

Promoted Pins take targeting to the next level by showing up in users' home feeds based on their interests and past browsing behavior. This personalized approach makes it more likely that users will engage with your ad. A/B testing and ongoing optimization are crucial for honing your Pinterest ad targeting. By testing different ad elements, such as images, headlines, and call-to-action buttons, you can find out which combinations work best for your audience. Analyzing your performance data and user engagement metrics will help you optimize your campaigns to get the best results and meet your marketing goals.

Creating Engaging Ads

Crafting Pinterest ads that seize the attention of your desired audience and compel them to act is pivotal for a triumphant advertising endeavor. The bedrock of compelling Pinterest ads is the presence of top-tier visuals. Employ captivating images or videos that spotlight your offerings in an arresting manner. Keep in mind that Pinterest is a platform that thrives on visuals, so ensure yours are of the highest quality. Keep your ad copy short

The bedrock of compelling Pinterest ads is the presence of top-tier visuals.

and sweet. It should work with your visuals to give people more information about your product. Use clear, compelling language that speaks to your target audience and fits your brand. A strong call to action is important to get people to do what you want them to do, whether that's visiting your site, making a purchase, or signing up for your newsletter.

Pinterest offers a variety of ad formats, including standard pins, video pins, carousel pins, and shopping pins. Test different formats to see what works best for your product or service. You can also choose where your ads appear, such as in-home feed, search results, or related pins. By selecting targeting options like keywords, interests, and demographics, you can make sure your ads are seen by the right people.

Tracking and Analyzing Performance

Pinterest provides analytics tools that offer valuable insights into ad performance. They typically aren't as robust as those on Meta or Google, but they still enable you to monitor key metrics such as impressions, clicks, conversions, and engagement rates.

In addition to Pinterest's analytics, you can use heatmaps to see how users interact with your ads. Heatmaps show you which areas of your ad get the most attention, which can help you optimize your ad design and messaging for better engagement. A/B testing is another great way to improve ad performance. By testing different ad variations, you can see which elements resonate best with your target audience and lead to more conversions.

Cons of Pinterest Ads:

Ad Creation and Management: The creation and management of Pinterest ads can be more complex than other social media platforms. The ad platform has unique features and requirements which may take some time to learn for businesses new to the platform. Ongoing management and optimization of Pinterest ad campaigns are essential to ensure optimal performance, which can be time-consuming and require specialized skills.

Limited Targeting Options: While Pinterest ads offer precise targeting capabilities, they may have fewer targeting options compared to other platforms like Facebook or Google. For businesses looking for extremely granular targeting based on specific demographics or behaviors, Pinterest may not provide the same level of customization as other platforms. However, Pinterest continues to enhance its targeting capabilities, and businesses can still achieve effective targeting by strategically leveraging the available options.

Pinterest ads can be a valuable platform for the right clinic or facility, especially for organic social posting. The return on investment for ads is much more diminished. Typically our experience is that repurposed content from Instagram to Pinterest is more effective in the mental or behavioral health marketing space than Pinterest ads. That being said, if you want to set aside some budget to experiment with Pinterest ads, we have found the platform to be a powerhouse in directing traffic to our clients' websites.

TikTok, Snapchat, and Reddit

In our experience at Beacon Media + Marketing, we found that these three social media channels have limited ROI for mental and behavioral health clinics. Yes, they have a lot of active users nationally and globally, but that doesn't always mean it is the right user or that a business has the time to invest, which is equal to the return for that time. Let's look at each one individually.

What is TikTok?

TikTok has taken the social media world by storm, capturing the attention of users around the globe. With over 1 billion active users, TikTok is now the seventh most popular social media platform in the world. This rapid growth is largely due to its appeal to Gen Z and Millennial users, who make up the majority of its user base. These users are known for their tech-savviness, creativity, and desire for authentic content. TikTok's user-friendly interface and focus on short-form videos have made it a hit with this audience.

What is Snapchat?

Snapchat is a popular multimedia messaging app that allows users to send photos, videos, and messages that disappear after being viewed. With features like filters, lenses, and stories, Snapchat provides a fun and interactive platform for communication and sharing moments with friends and followers. Users can also discover content from publishers, influencers, and brands in the Discover section, making it a versatile social media platform for connecting, creating, and exploring a wide range of content.

What is Reddit?

Reddit is a diverse online community platform where users can engage in discussions, share content, and discover a wide range of topics and interests. Known as the "front page of the internet," Reddit consists of thousands of user-created communities called subreddits, each focused on a specific theme or subject. Users can upvote or downvote posts and comments, leading to a dynamic ranking system that highlights popular content. With a mix of text posts, links, images, and videos, Reddit offers a unique space for users to connect, learn, and participate in conversations on virtually any topic imaginable.

All three of these platforms offer various forms of ads with targeting and analysis. TikTok and Snapchat primarily focus on younger Millennials and Gen Z demographics and require strong and frequently changing video and image-driven ads. Most facilities find it challenging to keep up with this from both a social media posting and ad creation standpoint. There are agencies and freelancers who specialize in these platforms for the clinics who want to try them out but don't want to handle it internally. However, the ROI from platforms like Meta, Google, YouTube, and LinkedIn typically far surpass those of these platforms combined.

Streaming Services & Podcast Ads

Advertising on streaming platforms like Netflix, Hulu, Amazon Prime, and HBO Max can offer numerous benefits for mental health clinics looking to enhance their marketing efforts. Here are some key advantages:

Targeted Reach: Streaming platforms allow for precise targeting based on user demographics, interests, viewing habits, and more. Mental health clinics can reach specific audiences who are more likely to be interested in their services, ensuring that their ads are seen by individuals who may benefit from mental health support.

Early Adoption Opportunity: Advertising on streaming services like Hulu, Netflix, Pandora, and Spotify is a rapidly growing trend, yet it's still in its early stages. This presents a unique opportunity for mental health clinics to be early adopters and get their brand in front of the right audiences while there is still low saturation by other clinics. Viewers often see the same ad replayed over and over during their programming, making it easier for innovative practices to stand out.

Brand Visibility: Advertising on popular streaming platforms can increase brand visibility and awareness for mental health clinics. With the potential to reach a large and diverse audience, clinics can establish their presence in the digital landscape and position themselves as trusted resources for mental health information and services.

Content Integration: Clinics can align their ads with relevant content on streaming platforms, ensuring that their messaging appears alongside shows or movies that share similar themes or target demographics. This strategic alignment can enhance the effectiveness of the ads and increase the likelihood of connecting with viewers who are seeking mental health resources.

Measurable Results: Streaming platforms provide robust analytics and tracking capabilities, allowing clinics to monitor the performance of their ads in real-time. By analyzing key metrics such as views, clicks, and conversions, clinics can optimize their campaigns for maximum impact and return on investment.

Overall, leveraging ads on popular streaming platforms can be a valuable marketing strategy for mental health clinics, providing a targeted, engaging, and measurable approach to reaching their desired audience and promoting their services in a digital-first world.

Podcasts as an Advertising Tool

In the realm of podcasts, mental and behavioral health clinics can explore various opportunities to integrate their messaging and expertise into the podcasting landscape. Clinics can sponsor mental health-focused podcasts, collaborate with podcast hosts to discuss relevant topics, or even create their own podcast series to share valuable insights and resources with listeners. By participating in the podcasting space, clinics cannot only share their expertise but also establish themselves as thought leaders in the mental health field, build relationships with podcast audiences, and attract new clients who resonate with their content.

Advertising during podcasts can offer several benefits for behavioral health clinics as part of their marketing strategy:

Targeted Audience: Podcasts often have niche audiences interested in specific topics, making them an ideal platform for clinics to reach individuals seeking mental health support or information. By selecting podcasts that align with their target demographic, clinics can effectively reach potential clients who are actively engaged in mental health conversations.

Trust and Credibility: Podcast listeners tend to have a strong connection with the hosts and content they listen to regularly. By advertising on podcasts, behavioral health clinics can leverage the trust and credibility established by podcast hosts to enhance their own brand reputation. Listeners are more likely to trust recommendations from podcast hosts they respect.

Brand Awareness: Advertising during podcasts can increase brand awareness for behavioral health clinics among a highly engaged and attentive audience. Listeners often develop a strong connection with the podcasts they follow, making podcast advertising an effective way to introduce clinics to new audiences and expand their reach in the mental health community.

Engagement and Impact: Podcast ads have the potential to meaningfully engage listeners as they are integrated into the natural flow of the podcast content. Clinics can create authentic and engaging ad scripts that resonate with listeners and prompt them to take action, whether visiting the clinic's website, scheduling a consultation, or seeking more information about their services.

Overall, leveraging podcast advertising can be a valuable marketing tactic for behavioral health clinics, offering a targeted, trusted, and engaging platform to connect with individuals.

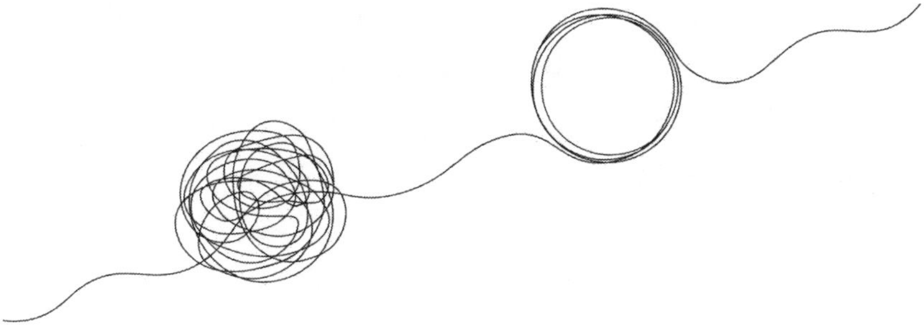

Chapter 8: Tips for Effective Video Marketing

More than likely, if you've been reading this book from the beginning, you've noticed video is a part of virtually every chapter. Video has become one of the most powerful tools in any digital marketing strategy. Shorts, reels, stories, whatever you call them, are incredibly effective at communicating complex messages, engaging viewers on an emotional level, and driving conversions. That being said, video is also one of the hardest elements of a marketing campaign. So, if you're struggling to get video implemented into your clinic's marketing plan, you're not alone.

In a moment, we're going to dig into all of the benefits of using video in marketing, but before we get there, let's go ahead and talk about the elephant in the room. VIDEO!

The truth is that it is very common for people to get intimidated by the idea of being on camera. And I'm not just talking about people who naturally prefer to be behind the scenes. Video is its own unique beast, and it can be hard even for people who are used to talking in front of people on a regular basis. In the same way that people critique and nitpick a photo of themselves to death, people struggle to see and hear themselves on camera.

So, if you're the one struggling with being on camera or you're trying to convince a supervisor or colleague that they need to embrace video, we'll start by talking about all the reasons why it's worth overcoming the fear of being on camera. Then, we'll dig into some ideas for doing the video anyway.

Video Improves Search Results

Videos rank higher than text-based content because they are more engaging and visually appealing to users. This means that users are more likely to click on them and watch them, which can improve your click-through rate (CTR). In addition, videos are great for reducing bounce rates. When you can captivate a viewer with a video, you can keep them on your site longer. This longer dwell time is a positive signal to search engines that your site has valuable and engaging information. As a result, your site will rank higher in search results, thereby potentially increasing the number of clients who could book an appointment.

By creating video content around specific keywords and phrases, you can directly target the terms that your audience is searching for. This can help you improve your organic search rankings, ensuring that your website appears at the top of the search results when potential customers are looking for mental health assistance.

Video Enhances the Customer Experience

In today's digital world, customers expect a personalized and engaging experience when interacting with your clinic or facility. Video content is uniquely positioned to meet these expectations and deliver an enhanced customer experience. Compared to traditional text-based content, videos capture attention, increase comprehension, and create a lasting impact on viewers.

Videos offer a more immersive and interactive way for you to engage with your clients. By integrating videos into your digital marketing strategies, you can create personalized and tailored content that speaks directly to your target audience. Videos enable clinics to present their services in a visually compelling way, making it easier for clients to understand and appreciate what they have to offer. Moreover, videos can be used to provide helpful information on mental health issues, increasing awareness around addiction, depression, suicide, and other issues.

By including calls-to-action within your videos, you can nudge your viewers to book an appointment, sign up for a service, or visit your website. Videos are also a great way to show customer reviews. These reviews help you build trust and credibility with your potential customers. The sight of real customers talking about their good experiences with your product or service can be very persuasive and change buying decisions. This gets a little tricker in the mental or behavioral health space due to HIPAA compliance issues, but it is still doable. That being said, video testimonials from current employees at various levels within your facility can be one of the most powerful tools in your recruitment marketing campaigns.

Video for Trust and Authenticity

Videos provide a way to tell real stories, helping you connect with your audience on a personal level. By sharing the stories behind the brand and its origin story, facilities like yours can evoke emotions and create a lasting impression on viewers. This emotional connection fosters trust and loyalty, transforming customers into brand advocates.

Moreover, videos provide your clinic with the chance to be transparent and give behind-the-scenes access. (Obviously, make sure your behind-the-scenes videos are HIPAA compliant.) This can help build a sense of authenticity and credibility, as you're giving customers a look into how your business operates. This transparency can help build trust and make customers feel more connected to your brand.

Videos are a powerful tool for building trust and authenticity in digital marketing. By showing real people, telling authentic stories, sharing customer testimonials, and being transparent, facilities can connect with their audience in a way that builds long-term trust and loyalty.

Video, the Most Social of all Content

Video content has become the most shared form of media on social platforms, with people more inclined to share videos with their networks than any other format. This presents a tremendous opportunity for clinics to expand their reach and grow their social media following.

Social media platforms recognize video content's power and actively promote it. For instance, Facebook and Instagram have given videos more prominence in users' feeds and introduced new features to facilitate video sharing. Consequently, facilities aiming for success on social media must ensure they create and share high-quality video content.

Not only are videos more likely to be shared, but they can also generate more leads and conversions than other forms of content. This is because videos can capture your audience's attention more effectively and for a longer period of time. This gives you more time to deliver your message and convince your audience to take action.

To ensure your video content on social media hits the mark, keep it short, sweet, and engaging. People are drawn to videos that are easy to watch and that amuse them. Authenticity is key—steer clear of content that feels forced or overly promotional. Your audience will be more likely to share content that feels genuine and relatable.

Video for Analytics and ROI

In addition to better analytics and a higher ROI, digital marketing has become more data-driven. This means that marketers can measure just about every aspect of their strategy, including video.

Through video, you can gain real-time insights into viewer behavior and engagement. Detailed analytics allow you to track user interactions, including watch time, click-through rates, and conversion rates. This makes it easier to measure the impact of your video content on your business goals and ROI.

A/B testing is another tool that can help you optimize your video content for maximum impact. By testing different video elements, such as length, thumbnail, and call-to-action placement, you can identify the most effective strategies to engage your target audience. The ability to track how users interact and click on your videos gives you important data for making smart decisions. This helps you ensure that your video content aligns with your business goals and gets the results you want.

Harnessing the power of video analytics gives you a leg up in the digital marketing game. With these data-driven insights, you can fine-tune your approach, optimize your video content, and achieve the best possible results. Video analytics enable you to make smart choices, allocate your resources wisely, and reach your digital marketing goals with precision and speed.

Video Resources

We want to share some resources we've found helpful for creating effective videos for your website and social media.

Visit this website for video guidelines, including www.beaconmm.com/digitalmarketingbook

- How to put together a storyboard and script for your video
- Microphone and lighting tips
- Editing programs

- Remote recording programs
- And more

Chapter 9: Additional Marketing Options

Online Reviews

For most companies, asking for reviews is a vital part of their business. For mental and behavioral health clinics, things get complicated. The American Psychological Association's Code of Ethics states, "Psychologists do not solicit testimonials from current therapy clients/patients or other persons who, because of their particular circumstances, are vulnerable to undue influence." This is a matter of professional integrity. This means you can't ask for a review or testimonial from a current client. That being said, there are still some options open to you, including:

- You can leave a business card-sized "review card" with a QR code to where you want people to leave a review in your waiting room or at the receptionist's desk. If people pick it up and leave a review, it is their own choice and not solicited.

- You can approach former clients for testimonials and reviews

---

The American Psychological Association's Code of Ethics states,
"Psychologists do not solicit testimonials from current therapy clients/patients or other persons who, because of their particular circumstances, are vulnerable to undue influence."

Additionally, you must be very careful how you respond to online reviews. According to HIPAA regulations, clients may disclose that they've received care at your facility, but you cannot confirm this in your response. You can thank them for the review, but that is it.

Conferences

Conferences and trade shows offer unique opportunities for mental and behavioral health companies as opposed to other industries. Typically, potential clients don't go to a conference or trade show to look for a therapist or an addiction recovery clinic for themselves or a loved one. But that doesn't mean conferences and trade shows aren't valuable for other reasons. Here are a few to consider:

Networking Opportunities: Conferences and trade shows provide a platform for mental health professionals to network with industry peers, experts, and potential partners. Engaging in face-to-face interactions can help build relationships, establish connections, and create opportunities for collaboration and referrals within the mental health community.

Brand Visibility: Exhibiting at industry-specific conferences and trade shows can increase brand visibility and raise awareness about mental health clinics' services, expertise, and offerings. By showcasing their presence at industry events, companies can attract the attention of attendees, generate interest in their services, and differentiate themselves from competitors.

Education and Thought Leadership: Conferences often feature speaker sessions, workshops, and panel discussions where mental health professionals can share their knowledge, insights, and expertise on relevant topics. Presenting at these events can position companies as thought leaders in the field, enhance their credibility, and demonstrate their commitment to advancing mental health awareness and education.

Lead Generation: Conferences and trade shows provide a valuable opportunity for mental health companies to generate leads and attract potential clients. By engaging with attendees, collecting contact information, and offering informative materials or resources, companies can cultivate relationships with individuals who may be interested in their services or seeking mental health support. Interestingly enough, this often comes from people who are attending the conference as vendors.

Market Research: Attending conferences and trade shows allows mental health companies to stay informed about industry trends, emerging technologies, and best practices in mental health care. Clinics can gain insights into the needs and preferences of their target audience, gather feedback on their services, and identify opportunities for innovation and growth within the mental health sector.

Overall, participating in conferences and trade shows can be a strategic and effective component of a marketing campaign for mental and behavioral health companies, offering opportunities for networking, brand visibility, education, lead generation, and market research to support their growth and success in the industry.

What types of print advertising are still effective?

In the digital age, it's easy to think of print advertising as a thing of the past. However, print advertising, such as magazines, newspapers, transit advertising, billboards, and direct mail, still has a place in the modern marketing mix.

Magazines

In the world of print advertising, magazine ads have long been a staple for businesses. Despite the growth of digital marketing and advertising, magazine ads have continued to be an effective way to reach consumers. This is because magazines are able to provide a unique and engaging reading experience that can't be replicated by digital media, allowing the reader to become fully immersed in the content and make the reading experience more enjoyable and memorable. Additionally, magazines are often seen as a more trustworthy source of information, which can help to build brand loyalty and trust with consumers.

Moreover, magazines offer a unique opportunity for targeted advertising. Unlike digital advertising, which can sometimes feel impersonal and intrusive, magazines usually cater to a very niche market. This targeted approach allows facilities to reach their desired audience with greater precision and relevance. Additionally, the physical nature of magazines ensures that ads are seen multiple times, increasing brand recall and recognition.

Newspapers

In the world of print advertising, newspapers were once the place to put your ad. But times have changed. With the rise of digital media, newspapers have faced significant challenges. While they can still be a great way to reach a local audience, there are a number of reasons why they may not be the best choice for your advertising dollars.

A key shortcoming of newspaper advertising is the challenge of tracking return on investment (ROI). Unlike digital advertising, which offers detailed metrics and analytics, newspapers do not have strong mechanisms in place to measure the impact of ads. This can make it difficult for businesses to understand the true value of their newspaper advertising investments.

Transit advertising

In the world of out-of-home (OOH) advertising, transit advertising is a powerful and cost-effective medium. It reaches people as they go about their day, often when they are away from home and near the point of purchase. Transit advertising can be found on buses, taxis, trains, subways, airports, and more. The main benefit of transit advertising is that it can't be turned off like a television, delivers a big, bold message, and can't be skipped over like a print ad.

The strategic placement of transit advertising ensures that you can target specific geographic areas with precision. This enables you to effectively reach customers within their local communities, tailoring your marketing efforts to the unique characteristics and preferences of each region.

It's important to note that transit advertising can be costly to produce, especially for short-term campaigns. To decide if it's the right strategy for your business, you'll need to weigh your marketing goals and budget against the potential benefits. But if you're looking to capture the attention of a large audience and make a big impact in your target market, transit advertising could be a powerful tool for your business.

Billboards

In the world of advertising, billboards are the closest thing to a visual giant. They are the beacon of light in a bustling city, strategically placed on highways and cityscapes to capture the attention of passersby, commuters, and pedestrians. With a large canvas, billboards communicate brand identity, promote products and services, and inspire action through the use of striking visuals, bold colors, and concise messaging.

The flexibility of billboards allows your clinic to customize your message to your exact audience, ensuring that your message is seen by the right people who are seeking mental health help. The power of billboards to make a lasting impression on consumers is their most enduring legacy. Their size and location make them impossible to ignore, and they are an ideal way to build brand recognition and create a strong brand image.

Direct Mail

In the world of print advertising, direct mail is the clear standout. It offers the unique ability to deliver targeted messages and provide measurable results. By leveraging data and market research, you can tailor your direct mail campaigns to target specific age groups, income levels, or even geographic locations. This targeted approach increases the likelihood of your message resonating with your audience and driving conversions.

Are TV and Radio Ads Still Effective?

In today's fast-paced media landscape, traditional advertising methods like TV and radio ads are facing significant challenges. With the continuous decline in viewership and the rise of innovative ad-blocking technologies, the effectiveness of these traditional channels is under scrutiny. However, the growth of streaming video services and streaming radio platforms has created new advertising opportunities with better targeting and engagement. So, the answer is no; radio and TV ads are no longer effective for mental or behavioral health clinics. Streaming Ads have replaced traditional TV and radio commercials and are much more powerful for clinics because they are cheaper to produce, and the tracking is accurate and helpful in measuring ROI.

Video ads for streaming videos

Platforms like YouTube, Hulu, and Netflix offer a range of video ad formats, each with its own advantages and drawbacks. Here, we'll explore some of the most common video ad formats and look at what makes each of them effective.

The **pre-roll ad** is one of the most popular video ad formats. It plays before the main content and is usually short, lasting anywhere from a few seconds to a minute. Viewers can often skip pre-roll ads after a certain amount of time. While pre-roll ads can be seen as intrusive, they give advertisers a chance to capture viewers' attention before they watch the main content.

Mid-roll ads, on the other hand, are longer and appear in the middle of the video. They may be more intrusive, but they also provide a unique opportunity to engage with viewers who are already invested in the content. However, if not executed thoughtfully, they can lead to viewers abandoning the video altogether.

In-stream ads are a versatile video ad format that can be integrated into the video content. They can be presented as sponsored content, product placements, or interactive overlays. Less intrusive than pre-roll and mid-roll ads, in-stream ads offer advertisers a platform for more creative and engaging storytelling.

The real-time performance tracking of video ads for streaming videos is a game-changer. With detailed analytics on impressions, clicks, engagement, and conversions, you can optimize your campaigns on the fly. This level of tracking and optimization is not easily achievable with traditional TV ads.

Video ads for streaming videos are a potent tool for reaching and engaging audiences. With a range of ad formats and targeting options, they can be tailored to specific campaign goals and target audiences. The ability to track performance in real-time further enhances the effectiveness of video ads, making them a valuable addition to any digital marketing strategy.

Ads on streaming radio services, such as Pandora and Spotify

Streaming radio services, such as Pandora and Spotify, have revolutionized the way we listen to music and podcasts and offer a variety of advertising options that can be highly effective in reaching your target audience.

Streaming radio services offer a range of ad formats, including audio ads, display ads, and video ads. Audio ads are the most common and are typically inserted between songs or during breaks in podcasts. Display ads are visual ads that appear on the user's screen, while video ads are short video clips that play before, during, or after audio content.

Ads on streaming radio services work better if they are in the right format, reach the right people, and can be targeted. Audio ads are very good at making people know and remember brands. Display and video ads are better at getting clicks and conversions. Streaming radio services also offer precise targeting options based on people's age, interests, and even their past listening history. This lets advertisers reach their desired audience more accurately.

One of the most compelling reasons to advertise on streaming radio services is the ability to track campaign performance in real-time. These platforms provide a wealth of tools and analytics to monitor impressions, clicks, conversions, and more. This data can be used to optimize campaigns and ensure they are delivering the desired results.

Therefore, streaming radio services like Pandora and Spotify offer many powerful advertising options for businesses of all sizes. With a range of ad formats, pinpoint targeting capabilities, and robust tracking and analytics tools, these platforms offer an exceptional opportunity to connect with your audience and propel business expansion.

Grassroots Marketing

Network marketing is a dynamic business model that has been around for decades and has helped many companies grow their customer base and revenue. By building a network of loyal customers and business partners, you can increase your visibility, generate leads, and build long-lasting relationships with your customers. In this blog post, we'll look at the different types of network marketing strategies, how they work, and what you need to do to make them work for you. We'll look at ways to grow your business, from talking to people in person to groups of friends and local marketing campaigns.

Face-to-Face Marketing and Word-of-Mouth Marketing

In network marketing, face-to-face marketing is one of the most direct and personal ways to connect with potential clients. This method involves proactively engaging with people, having conversations, and introducing them to your products or services. By doing this, you can build rapport, answer questions, and create a relationship that goes beyond a simple transaction.

Word-of-mouth marketing, by contrast, leverages the power of satisfied clients and their personal endorsements. When your clients are thrilled with their experience, they become your biggest fans, telling their friends, family, and colleagues about your facility. This organic form of marketing is built on trust, credibility, and great service. By consistently exceeding expectations, you can create a chain reaction of positive word-of-mouth that will help you reach new clients without spending a fortune on advertising.

Both face-to-face marketing and word-of-mouth marketing offer cost-effective advantages. Face-to-face interactions don't need expensive advertising campaigns, allowing businesses to spend money on improving their products or services. Similarly, word-of-mouth marketing relies on the unpaid endorsements of satisfied customers, making it a budget-friendly yet impactful strategy.

Networking Groups

Networking groups, such as Business Network International (BNI), provide a structured environment for businesses to meet, collaborate, and grow. BNI is a global organization with chapters in over 70 countries, and it offers access to a wide range of professionals from various industries. Membership in BNI includes regular meetings, usually once a week, where members exchange ideas, leads, and business referrals. This structured approach to networking creates a sense of responsibility and encourages members to actively support each other's businesses.

The effectiveness of networking groups like BNI is contingent upon the commitment and engagement of their members. By actively participating in meetings, contributing to the group's goals, and building strong relationships, businesses can leverage the power of networking to drive growth and success.

Local marketing groups are a fantastic resource for businesses looking to network and grow. These groups often organize events, workshops, and meetings to help members connect, share ideas, and collaborate. Attending these events is a great way to meet potential customers, partners, and mentors who can provide valuable insights and opportunities. Additionally, participating in local networking organizations, such as the Chamber of Commerce, can offer access to a broader network and resources specifically tailored to local businesses.

Collaborating with complementary businesses can help expand your reach and provide access to clients. For example, if you are a therapist who specializes in children, you could build a solid referral relationship with a pediatrician or a school counselor. Also, a company that specializes in sober companions could cultivate referral partnerships with clinics to offer them as an option for people getting out of recovery.

Marketing Through Local Groups like the Chamber of Commerce

Engaging with local groups such as the Chamber of Commerce or Rotary can be a strategic move for facilities aiming to broaden their local community connections. Active participation in Chamber or rotary activities can greatly enhance your clinic's visibility and reputation. By joining committees, volunteering for leadership roles and attending events, you can make new business contacts, share your expertise and establish your company as a community leader.

When considering grassroots marketing, it is important to consider the amount of time key employees have to commit to the endeavor. As with most marketing initiatives, consistency is key!

Chapter 10: The Marketing Strategy

Now, it's time to put everything you've learned into a cohesive strategy that you and your team can implement! In this final chapter, we'll look at how to integrate all of the elements in the first nine chapters, how to plan out campaigns, and how to measure the ROI of your efforts!

Your marketing strategy should incorporate the following components:

- Marketing Why and Goals
- Branding Standards
    - Logo, font, colors, etc
    - Company messaging and values
- Target Audience Profiles
- Your Website
- Content Marketing Goals
- Social Media Goals
- Paid Ads Goals

- Plan for any Additional Marketing Efforts
- Rhythm for Reviewing and Editing Your Campaigns

This document acts as a guide for everything else you do in marketing. You will refer back to it extensively, and it should be your true north throughout the year as you measure your analytics and decide what is working and what needs tweaking.

Campaign Timing

We recommend that you review and update your main marketing strategy annually. Some years, you may significantly update your website, social media, or paid ads goals. In other years, you might just tweak parts depending on their effectiveness.

Once you are comfortable with your overall strategy, then you need to break it down into 90-day or 6-month campaign arcs or sprints. These smaller campaigns have specific seasonal themes, like focusing on seasonal affective disorder (SAD) symptoms in the winter. These arcs should include goals around your focus and bring together all of the channels you want to use. Typically, you want to create specific videos and graphics around the theme in the campaign sprint, and it should run just during the agreed-upon time frame.

Once the designated time is coming to an end, it is important to evaluate the campaign data so you and your team are well-informed about what is working and what is not when you plan your next campaign.

Evergreen Assets

Some of the most powerful tools for any marketer are evergreen assets. These assets are typically focused on branding or services your facility always offers and don't age out. You can use these assets month after month, year after year, and pepper them into your shorter campaign arcs for brand continuity.

Elements of a Successful Marketing Strategy

Know Why You're Marketing and Your Brand

To start off, understand why you're marketing; it is often more intricate than just wanting new clients.

- Expanding market share in a specific geography or specialty (you're looking to get the majority of the clients out there who need you)
- Launching or relaunching a new specialty
- Increasing awareness of your clinic (your brand) or to build brand credibility
- Attract and retain top talent
- Generate potential partnerships or investors
- Get more clients

Next, a strong brand identity is the foundation of any successful marketing strategy. This section will help you define your brand, its mission and values, and what makes it unique. By understanding your brand's DNA, you can create a cohesive and compelling marketing strategy that resonates with your target audience and sets you apart from the competition.

Define your Target Audience

At the heart of any successful marketing strategy is a deep understanding of your target audience. You need to know who your potential clients are and what they care about. This is the only way to create marketing campaigns that will resonate with them. To do this, you need to learn as much as you can about your clients' demographics, psychographics, decision-making habits, and preferences.

Let's start with the basics. Demographics are the quantifiable statistics of a given population. This includes age, gender, location, occupation, income, and education level. Next, delve into psychographics to discover the deeper motivations and values behind your client's actions. What are their interests, hobbies, and passions? What do they care about most? By understanding these aspects, you can create marketing messages that resonate on a personal level, which can help you strengthen your connection with your customers and foster brand loyalty.

Remember, your target audience is the compass guiding your marketing journey. By understanding them deeply, you can create marketing campaigns that speak directly to their hearts and minds, driving business growth and building a loyal customer base.

Identify your Competition

To create a marketing strategy that will be successful, it's important to understand the competition. Start by identifying your direct competitors, those who offer similar products or services in the same geographic area. Then, take a close look at their strengths and weaknesses, market share, pricing strategies, and reputation with customers. This will give you a good idea of what you're up against and what you can do to differentiate your business.

Next, delve into the unique selling propositions (USPs) of your rivals. What makes them the go-to choice for customers? By pinpointing the features, benefits, or customer experiences that set them apart, you can identify the gaps in the market and craft your own distinct positioning.

In addition, take a close look at your competitors' social media channels, content marketing strategies, and online reviews. This will give you a good idea of how they're marketing their products, how they're engaging with their audience, and what their customers are saying about them. By doing this, you'll be able to create better marketing campaigns and improve your online reputation.

In conclusion, a thorough competitive analysis will arm you with the knowledge you need to make smarter decisions, target your marketing efforts more effectively, and position your small business for success in a competitive marketplace.

Set Clear Business Goals

Measuring the success of your marketing efforts and making necessary adjustments is crucial for sustained growth. By regularly monitoring website traffic and user behavior using tools like Google Analytics, you gain valuable insights into your audience's preferences and engagement. Analyze metrics like bounce rates, time spent on site, and conversion rates to identify areas for improvement.

In addition, monitor social media interactions and consider conducting surveys to gather direct customer feedback. This information can be invaluable, providing you with a clear understanding of your audience's needs, concerns, and preferences. By aligning your marketing strategy accordingly, you can ensure that your efforts are as effective as possible. Furthermore, tracking sales and conversion data will allow you to measure the success of your marketing campaigns.

Regularly reviewing and adjusting your marketing strategy based on data-driven insights is key to continuous growth. Embrace a data-driven mindset and use analytics to optimize your efforts, ensuring your marketing strategy remains relevant, effective, and aligned with your business goals.

Choose the Right Marketing Channels

With a clearly defined target audience and a deep understanding of their preferences and behaviors, the next step in building a successful marketing strategy is selecting the right marketing channels. This involves identifying the platforms and methods that will most effectively reach and engage your target audience, allowing you to communicate your brand message and drive desired actions.

There are many marketing channels available to small businesses, each with its own strengths and potential impact. Content marketing involves creating and sharing valuable, relevant, and consistent content to attract and retain a clearly defined audience. This can include blog posts, videos, infographics, podcasts, and more. Email marketing allows for direct communication with customers and can be highly personalized, making it an effective tool for building relationships and driving conversions.

Social media is another powerful tool at your disposal. Platforms like Facebook, YouTube, and Instagram offer a more personal and interactive way to connect with your audience. They let you share updates, engage in conversations, and build a community around your brand. And don't forget about paid advertising through Google AdWords or Facebook Ads. This can be a highly effective way to reach a specific audience and increase your visibility online.

Equally essential is the role of video advertising in captivating and compellingly conveying brand messages to your audience. By utilizing platforms like YouTube and Vimeo, you can share product videos, tutorials, and other visually engaging content. Don't underestimate the power of grassroots marketing strategies, such as networking and community sponsorships. These methods allow you to connect with your local community and potential customers in a more personal and direct manner.

By carefully considering the available marketing channels and selecting the ones that best align with your target audience, your business goals, and your budget, you can effectively reach your target audience and achieve your marketing objectives. Whether it's through content marketing, email marketing, social media, paid advertising, video advertising, or grassroots marketing, the key is to create a cohesive and integrated marketing strategy that leverages the strengths of each channel to maximize impact and drive growth.

Create a Content Marketing Plan

A well-structured content marketing plan is key to keeping your audience engaged. Start by creating a content calendar that maps out what, when, and where you'll publish your content. This calendar should be in line with your overall marketing goals and provide a clear path to content creation. Diversify your content types to include blog posts, videos, infographics, social media posts, and email newsletters. This variety will keep your audience engaged and allow you to reach them on different platforms.

When it comes to promoting your content, a mix of organic and paid strategies can be most effective. Share your content on social media, submit it to relevant industry directories and websites, and consider influencer marketing to help spread the word. You can also use email marketing to nurture your subscriber base and drive traffic to your website. Be sure to track and analyze the performance of your content using website analytics tools. Keep an eye on key metrics like website traffic, engagement rates, and conversion rates to understand what's resonating with your audience and make data-driven improvements to your content marketing strategy.

By implementing a well-executed content marketing plan, you can establish your business as a thought leader in your industry, attract and retain customers, and ultimately drive business growth.

Know your Current Stats

In today's competitive digital landscape, website analytics are a must-have for businesses looking to understand their customers and optimize their marketing strategies. By utilizing the data provided by website analytics platforms, you can get a comprehensive understanding of your website's performance and user behavior, allowing you to make data-driven decisions that drive growth and improve customer engagement.

Key performance indicators (KPIs) such as traffic volume, conversion rates, traffic sources, popular pages, and bounce rates provide valuable insights into how your website is performing and where improvements can be made. By analyzing these metrics, you can identify trends, patterns, and areas of success, as well as pinpoint areas that require attention. This knowledge empowers you to allocate resources effectively, optimize your website for a better user experience, and implement targeted marketing campaigns that resonate with your audience.

Moreover, website analytics are your compass in the ever-changing landscape of marketing. By monitoring your website's traffic and conversions before, during, and after a new campaign, you can quickly adjust your strategy to ensure the best results. This data-driven approach to marketing will help you stay ahead of the competition and reach your business goals.

Measure your Results and Adjust your Strategy

Measuring the success of your marketing efforts and making necessary adjustments is crucial for sustained growth. By regularly monitoring website traffic and user behavior using tools like Google Analytics, you gain valuable insights into your audience's preferences and engagement. Analyze metrics such as page views, bounce rates, and time spent on different pages to identify areas for improvement and optimize your website for better user experience.

In addition, monitoring social media interactions, such as likes, comments, shares, and mentions, is key to gauging the effectiveness of your social media campaigns. Surveys and polls are also effective tools for gathering customer feedback, as they provide you with direct input that can help you better understand your customers' needs and expectations.

Finally, scrutinize your sales and conversion data to gauge the impact of your marketing initiatives. Keep a watchful eye on key performance indicators (KPIs) such as conversion rates, cost per acquisition, and customer lifetime value. By aligning your marketing strategies with sales outcomes, you can make informed choices that will help you allocate resources wisely and optimize your return on investment.

Keep in mind that marketing is not a static process but a dynamic one, requiring your vigilance and adaptability. Regularly scrutinize your outcomes, spot trends, and tweak your marketing strategy as needed. This data-driven approach will ensure that your marketing remains in sync with the ever-changing needs and preferences of your target audience, propelling your small business to continuous growth and success.

How to Measure your ROI

Marketing ROI measures the revenue generated from your marketing campaigns relative to their cost. Understanding marketing ROI helps you assess your strategies and optimize your budget. You'll find worksheets for the formulas in this section at www.beaconmm.com/digitalmarketingbook

Understanding Marketing ROI

Marketing ROI quantifies the revenue generated by a marketing campaign in relation to its cost. It showcases the return on investment from diverse marketing programs, enabling businesses to:

- Validate their marketing expenditure by showing the revenue produced by these initiatives
- Assess the effectiveness of marketing strategies
- Make data-driven decisions about where to allocate time and budget

This metric is crucial for businesses to measure the success of their marketing efforts and optimize their strategies.

A precise calculation of marketing ROI aids in comprehending how marketing activities contribute to total revenue generation. It helps businesses optimize their budget allocation for future marketing campaigns by identifying which strategies and channels drive the most sales. There are different types of marketing ROI metrics, including:

- Cost per acquisition (CPA)
- Sales cycle days
- Engagement duration
- Customer lifetime value (CLTV)

Each of these metrics provides unique insights into the effectiveness of various marketing efforts.

Customer lifetime value (CLV) is a particularly important metric in marketing ROI. It represents the total worth of a customer's business over their entire relationship with the company and offers a long-term perspective on marketing investments. A focus on CLV enables businesses to formulate better decisions regarding customer acquisition and retention strategies, catalyzing sustainable profit and revenue growth.

Calculating Marketing ROI

To calculate marketing ROI, the basic formula is (Net Profit / Total Investment) X 100. This formula involves dividing the net profit generated by a marketing campaign by the total costs incurred and then multiplying by 100 to get a percentage. This simple yet powerful formula provides a clear picture of how much profit is being generated for every dollar spent on marketing, allowing you to measure marketing ROI effectively.

To calculate marketing ROI,
the basic formula is
(Net Profit / Total Investment) X 100.

Yet, elements like customer acquisition cost (CAC) and customer lifetime value (CLV) must be taken into account when computing marketing ROI. For instance, the Customer Lifetime Value ROI can be calculated using the formula (Customer Lifetime Value—

Marketing Investment) / Marketing Investment. By incorporating these metrics, businesses can gain a deeper understanding of the long-term impact of their marketing efforts and make more strategic decisions about where to invest their resources.

The Customer Lifetime Value ROI can be calculated using the formula
(Customer Lifetime Value - Marketing Investment) / Marketing Investment

---

Key metrics in calculating marketing ROI include:

- customer acquisition cost (CAC)
- average gross margin
- marketing cost

These metrics help determine the efficiency of different marketing channels and campaigns. By focusing on these metrics, businesses can identify high-performing strategies and optimize their marketing efforts for better results while keeping marketing costs in check.

Precise ROI measurement is pivotal in guiding data-driven decisions, fostering sustainable profit and revenue growth, and focusing marketing ROI measurements.

Ideal Marketing ROI Benchmarks

A good rule of thumb for marketing ROI is to aim for a ratio of 5:1. This means that for every dollar spent on the marketing budget, the business should generate five dollars in revenue. Achieving this ratio ensures that marketing efforts are profitable and justify the investment. However, bear in mind that this benchmark may fluctuate based on the industry and particular business objectives.

An exceptional marketing ROI ratio is typically around 10:1. While this level of return is considered outstanding, it isn't always attainable or necessary for every business. The key is to set realistic benchmarks based on industry standards and continuously strive to improve marketing efficiency. Aiming for a solid marketing ROI allows businesses to make knowledgeable decisions regarding their marketing strategies and budget allocation.

> *A good rule of thumb for marketing ROI is to aim for a ratio of 5:1. This means that for every dollar spent on the marketing budget, the business should generate five dollars in revenue.*

Real-world Examples of Marketing ROI

Real-world examples can provide valuable insights into how businesses have successfully optimized their marketing strategies to achieve high ROI. For instance, content marketing has proven to be highly effective, costing 62% less than traditional marketing methods while generating three times as many leads. Businesses that allocate a significant portion of their marketing budgets to content marketing often report high success levels. In fact, over 67% of marketers report generating business demand or leads from their content marketing efforts.

Personalized marketing is another powerful strategy for boosting ROI. DirectTV, for example, used demographic data to personalize its homepage for new movers, increasing user engagement despite offering fewer incentives. Similarly, Very.co.uk personalized website banners using customer information and weather data, resulting in increased relevance and engagement. These examples highlight the importance of leveraging data to create targeted and personalized marketing campaigns.

Behavior-triggered email campaigns are also effective in improving ROI. Many SaaS companies use these campaigns to re-engage users, resulting in higher completion rates for sign-ups and setups. A winter apparel store combined sales and weather data to pinpoint the best times for promotions, significantly improving its advertising effectiveness. These real-world examples demonstrate how data-driven decisions and targeted campaigns can lead to exceptional marketing ROI and inform future campaigns.

Challenges in Measuring Marketing ROI

Measuring marketing ROI can present challenges due to a myriad of factors. One of the main challenges is the complexity of attributing revenue to specific marketing touches, especially in multi-touch scenarios where multiple interactions contribute to a sale. Additionally, marketing effects often occur over extended periods, making it difficult to attribute results to specific campaigns.

Another challenge is connecting the dots between marketing campaigns and the achievement of marketing goals. Running multiple campaigns simultaneously complicates tracking spending and performance for each individual campaign. Establishing a baseline for calculating incremental value delivered by marketing is also a critical yet complex factor.

In the subsections that follow, we will examine the specific challenges encountered in multi-touch attribution and omnichannel campaign measurement in greater detail.

Complexity in Multi-touch Attribution

Multi-touch attribution involves tracking multiple customer touchpoints, which complicates accurate ROI measurement. Different attribution models, such as:

- 'last click'
- 'first click'
- 'linear'
- 'time decay'
- 'position-based'
- 'data-driven'

distribute credit differently across touchpoints, each with its pros and cons. Choosing the right model significantly impacts the perceived marketing ROI.

Direct revenue attribution assigns all revenue from a sale to a single marketing touch, while indirect attribution distributes the revenue across multiple touches, adding further complexity to accurately measure ROI. The challenge lies in selecting an attribution model that accurately reflects the contribution of various marketing efforts to the overall revenue.

Omnichannel Campaign Measurement

Omnichannel campaigns require integrating data from various online and offline channels, which complicates the process of accurately measuring ROI. For example, 60% of marketers measure the success of their social media activity based on the sales it generates. However, integrating data from different channels and ensuring consistency in measurement can be challenging.

Accurate ROI measurement in omnichannel campaigns involves using advanced analytics tools and establishing a consistent sales baseline. By focusing on both online and offline measurements, businesses can gain a comprehensive view of their marketing performance and make more informed decisions about their campaigns.

Best Practices for Accurate Marketing ROI Measurement

Adoption of best practices for measuring marketing ROI can considerably enhance accuracy and insights. One key practice is defining specific, measurable KPIs early on, which helps track and measure the success of marketing campaigns. Utilizing analytics tools, such as Google Analytics or Cyfe, can track cost per acquisition and other crucial metrics.

Segmenting marketing activities allows for easier tracking of ROI by measuring metrics for each specific activity separately. Creating a measurement dashboard with key marketing metrics helps in achieving sales goals by tracking activities like email subscribers, social media followers, and inbound calls. Holistic measurement frameworks that combine financial and non-financial metrics provide a more comprehensive view of marketing's impact.

Tracking the customer journey and focusing on KPIs like cost per acquisition and customer lifetime value can provide a detailed understanding of marketing ROI. Additionally, using share-of-voice metrics, such as PR and social media impressions, can offer insights into the broader impact of marketing campaigns.

Justifying Marketing Spend

Providing evidence of an effective marketing ROI is pivotal for validating marketing budgets and guaranteeing continuous investment in marketing strategies. By accurately calculating the ROI of current efforts, marketers can:

- Prove the effectiveness of their campaigns
- Justify their budgetary needs to executives
- Ensure continued investment in marketing initiatives that drive revenue and growth

This evidence-based approach ensures continued investment in a marketing strategy that supports future marketing efforts, driving revenue and sales growth while considering the sales growth marketing cost.

Aligning marketing efforts with sales teams' needs and goals creates a seamless customer journey that drives conversions. For example, Hubspot retargets website visitors based on their behavior to address common objections and encourage completion of sign-ups. By demonstrating the tangible results of marketing efforts, businesses can secure the necessary resources to sustain and expand their marketing strategies.

Optimizing Marketing Efforts Based on ROI Insights

Enhancing marketing efforts based on ROI insights entails focusing on the appropriate audience and fostering a culture of perpetual optimization. ROI data helps marketers allocate budgets properly by identifying high-performing channels and strategies. For instance, maximizing ROI in B2B marketing involves making data-driven decisions that align with business goals.

Marketers can use data from paid advertising campaigns to enhance SEO by identifying the most profitable keywords. Measuring customer interactions and sentiment on social media can highlight the effectiveness of marketing strategies. Focusing on long-term impact, such as brand awareness and customer lifetime value, helps track the overall success of marketing efforts.

Adopting a culture of continuous optimization and iteration based on data and insights is necessary for maximizing ROI. By regularly analyzing performance and making adjustments, businesses can ensure their marketing efforts remain effective and aligned with their goals.

Monitoring Marketing ROI in Real-Time

Real-time monitoring of marketing ROI with the aid of analytics tools can yield valuable insights and facilitate data-driven decisions. Tools like Google Analytics help track metrics such as top traffic sources, bounce rates, and conversions. MarketingCloudFX, powered by IBM Watson, tracks leads, phone calls, and email campaigns, offering a comprehensive view of marketing performance.

Some useful tools for marketers are:

- Kissmetrics: allows tracking user behavior across different devices, tying data back to real people, which aids in understanding customer journeys
- BuzzSumo: tracks social media metrics such as brand mentions, keywords, and content engagement, helping

marketers measure the impact of their social media activities.

- SEMrush and Ahrefs: provide SEO analytics, including keyword performance and competitor analysis, essential for optimizing marketing strategies

These tools can greatly optimize marketing efforts, enhancing their overall performance.

By leveraging these tools, businesses can gain real-time insights into their marketing efforts, justify their spend, and optimize campaigns for better results.

Resources for Further Learning

For individuals seeking a deeper understanding of marketing ROI, numerous resources can offer valuable insights. These resources offer comprehensive guidance on understanding and improving marketing ROI.

- '*Marketing ROI: The Path to Campaign, Customer, and Corporate Profitability*' by James D. Lenskold is a highly recommended read on this topic.
- '*Lean Analytics*' by Alistair Croll and Benjamin Yoskovitz focuses on metrics and analytics, including ROI.
- 'KPI Checklists' by Bernie Smith
- '*Measuring Marketing: 103 Key Metrics Every Marketer Needs*' by John Davis.

In conclusion, measuring marketing ROI is essential for assessing the effectiveness of marketing campaigns and making informed decisions about budget allocation and strategy adjustments. By understanding the key concepts, challenges, and best practices, businesses can optimize their marketing efforts and achieve better results. Remember, continuous optimization based on data and insights is crucial for maximizing ROI and driving long-term success. Embrace these strategies, and watch your marketing efforts soar!

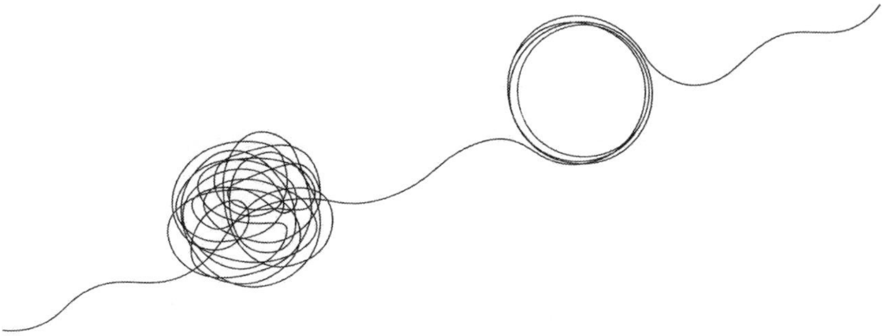

Conclusion

No matter the size of your business, you must have marketing to maintain or grow. However, the world of marketing, while more accessible, is also crowded and extremely noisy. In the midst of the chaos, the path through is about sticking to the basics, those foundational principles that don't really change even when the tools do.

I hope this book helps you focus despite the free-for-all that is modern marketing and work through the things that matter.

- Know why you're marketing
- Know who you're marketing to
- Your website is the hub of your marketing
- Pick your tools based on who you're marketing to
- Put together your strategy and be consistent

My hope is that the information and resources in this book will help you get your marketing off the ground or take it to the next level. I hope you fold corners, highlight points that resonate, make notes and scribble down ideas in the white space of this book, and it becomes a tool that helps you navigate through the perplexing and enigmatic world of marketing your business.

If you have questions that weren't answered, I would love to get feedback for future updates to this book because you know those will be needed. You can send questions to publishing@beaconmm.com, and I will make every effort to address them via blogs at www.beaconmm.com/blog/or podcasts or in future updates to this book.

If you want editable, downloadable versions of the forms in this book, you can find them at www.beaconmm.com/digitalmarketingbook. And if you've decided all of this sounds great but would rather partner with an agency to do it, we get that. We would love to chat about your goals and dreams for your business or organization. You can reach us at www.beaconmm.com/contact-us, email us at hello@beaconmm.com, or give us a call at 855-208-4312.

And that is the end of this book and the beginning of the next chapter of your marketing journey!

Made in the USA
Monee, IL
12 November 2026

e9260aed-620f-412c-a50c-30c29620a271R01